SECRETS OF SUCCESS IN YOUR OWN BUSINESS

SECRETS OF SUCCESS
IN YOUR OWN BUSINESS

by James L. Silvester

Lyle Stuart Inc.   Secaucus, New Jersey

Library of Congress Cataloging-in-Publication Data

Silvester, James L.
   Secrets of success in your own business.

   Includes index.
   1. Success in business.   2. Entrepreneur.
I. Title.
HF5386.S449 1986   658.4'2   86-14488
ISBN 0-8184-0418-3

Published by Lyle Stuart Inc.
120 Enterprise Ave., Secaucus, N.J. 07094
In Canada: Musson Book Company
A division of General Publishing Co. Limited.
Don Mills, Ontario

Queries regarding rights and permissions should be
addressed to: Lyle Stuart, 120 Enterprise Avenue,
Secaucus, N.J. 07094

Manufactured in the United States of America

I dedicate this book to my mother
RUTH A. SILVESTER
to whom I owe so much.

Acknowledgments

I would like to thank the many fine students who assisted in collecting much of the research that greatly added to the value of this book. Also, I wish to thank the organizations that gave their permission for use of the charts, tables, and research contained herein. In addition, gratitude is extended to my fine secretary, Pat Tharp, who typed the manuscript for this book. Not only did Pat correct my misspellings and incorrect grammar, but she also had to work with my idiosyncratic writing style, which, according to some, is an impossible task. Credit must also be extended to the fine people at Lyle Stuart, Inc., who allowed my creative energies to flow unencumbered by editorial intervention and for investing time and financial resources in this project.

Introduction

Without a doubt, the American economy has entered a period in which the entrepreneur is reigning supreme. Entrepreneurs have contributed much more to the economic scorecard than other elements of the business community. While large corporations have been busy reducing their work forces and product lines, entrepreneurial enterprises have created most of the growth in the country's employment and are responsible for many new inventions and product innovations.

Even though it is clear that the broad climate for entrepreneurial pursuits will improve over the coming decades, you should not overlook the individual factors that contribute to success. In this regard, I present this book and wish you the utmost success in your efforts to achieve economic independence.

—Professor James L. Silvester
Harry F. Byrd, Jr. School of Business
Shenandoah College
Winchester, Virginia 22601

Foreword

Have you ever wondered if you could start your own business and carve out your niche in the market place? Have you asked yourself, "Can I make my dreams a reality?"

Secrets of Success in Your Own Business is for you, if you've ever thought about the benefits of being an entrepreneur.

Entrepreneurs are the new buzz word in American business. Their faces appear on the covers of our news and business magazines and on network news shows. These adventurous souls are the new model of American success.

While entrepreneurship dominates discussions of our economy, our international competitiveness and our future, the character of the entrepreneur has remained elusive. The "nature of the beast" has gone undefined.

Jim Silvester set out to identify the characteristics of the successful entrepreneur and his informative work provides the best summary yet. It vastly increases our understanding of the "Homo Economicus" of the late twentieth century.

Not only does Professor Silvester identify most entrepreneurial traits, he provides the tools enabling the reader to ascertain how close he or she comes to the model. Professor Silvester's research permits aspiring entrepreneurs to compare their talents with those who have already attained a lofty goal.

And should you decide to test your skills in the marketplace—to take those risks which result in substantial rewards—Professor Silvester provides sound practical advice about business success.

In these pages you'll find guidance on the attitudes that make for business success and the techniques that lead to growth and prosperity.

In sum, *Secrets of Success in Your Own Business* is an accessible way to evaluate your own abilities and provides valuable advice to those who want to make the American dream their reality.

Paul Trible
United States Senator from Virginia

Preface

This book begins with a discussion of the basic individual characteristics that are needed to ensure entrepreneurial success. A test is
provided to measure your ability to survive in a self-employment
environment. Later chapters deal more specifically with the various
human traits that seem to predominate among successful entrepreneurs. The final part of the book directs itself to the emergence
of trends that entrepreneurs will have to deal with in the future.

Information found in this book is supported by painstaking research.
Many successful entrepreneurs were queried and interviewed, and
their conclusions are incorporated here. In addition, the various
experiences of consulting firms, venture capitalists, and academicians
associated with entrepreneurship have been used to support many
concepts outlined in the book. Names have been selectively changed to
protect the anonymity of those researched. However, if a particular
media requests access to the raw research, it will be allowed contingent
upon the guarantee that anonymity of those researched will be
maintained.

In addition, I do not proclaim to be an entrepreneur myself. The
information in this book is based on research and my personal
experiences as a management consultant to small and medium-sized
firms. Besides operating my consulting business, I serve on the faculty
of the Harry F. Byrd, Jr. School of Business at Shenandoah College,
teaching courses in various subjects including entrepreneurship. My
duties include managing the school's Small Business Institute. Also, I
sit on the board of directors of two small companies, one in the
communications field and the other serving the medical products
market.

It should be mentioned that a great debate is currently taking place among academicians, politicians, and researchers as to the meaning of the word "entrepreneur." Many experts distinguish between small businesses and entrepreneurial firms. These individuals contend that stable small firms are not entrepreneurial in nature because they are not oriented toward high growth, nor are they prone to invent new products/services. Their position is somewhat supported by the fact that only 10 percent of the country's small firms are responsible for most of the country's employment growth. They only see these job-generating small enterprises as entrepreneurial in nature. Now, according to Webster's Dictionary an entrepreneur is "one who organizes, manages, and assumes the risks of a business or enterprise." Who am I to disagree with Webster? I think it would be safe to say that any person who risks time and personal resources in pursuit of the creation of wealth should be given the honor of being called "entrepreneur." Whether an individual is running the small independent grocery store on the corner or embarking upon the creation of a new and revolutionary communications system, he/she has societal contributions to make. The communications system may create new jobs and make life easier and less costly for all of us. Likewise, that small grocery also has a role to play. It adds to the competitive stock in America which guarantees a marketplace free of restraint.

Food for Thought

Big and Bad

With so much attention in this country being focused on large corporations buying each other and on the concentration of assets, it is very interesting to compare the economic and societal impact of large versus small companies.

To the chagrin of the *Fortune* 500, American entrepreneurship has risen like a phoenix from oblivion, proudly proclaiming its contribution to the economy and projecting itself as the protector of American economic freedoms. Without a doubt, its track record is persuasive, if not downright formidable.

While many large enterprisees have been floundering without a focus or resolve, small companies have been busy producing jobs by the millions and introducing new products, processes, and services at a record rate. According to President Reagan's report to Congress on small business, between 1980 and 1982 firms with fewer than twenty employees created 2.6 million jobs, offsetting the loss of approximately 1.7 million jobs in larger businesses. The study acknowledged that "in virtually every industry between 1980 and 1982, overall employment grew in small firms and declined in large firms."

In addition, a Federal Trade Commission research report has concluded that small businesses produced 86 percent of all new jobs in the 1970s. Most of the remaining 14 percent was attributed to the growth in local, state, and federal governments. Even though the Brookings Institute has somewhat disputed such findings, a recently published report stated that the nation's largest one thousand companies generated only 122,000 jobs out of the total 20 million created in the last decade.

15

These points can be driven home by taking a look at the giant Du Pont Corporation. According to *Forbes* magazine, in 1983 Du Pont increased its profits by 26 percent, but at the same time the company reduced its employment rolls by 9000 individuals. Also, Ford Motor Company recently announced that it plans to eliminate 20 percent of its white-collar work force by 1990, and AT&T has also made public its plan to reduce employment by 24,000 jobs at one of its larger divisions. Eastman Kodak is also following suit by proclaiming the intention to reduce its worldwide employment by 10 percent, and U.S. Steel is chopping 15 percent of its staff positions.

Without a doubt, the scorecard is clear—small is better. Renowned management expert Peter Drucker summed it up perfectly in a recent interview with *U. S. News and World Report* by stating that "there is no longer a premium on big size. . . . "

With such overwhelming evidence glaring in the face of our nation's decision makers, why the foot dragging when it comes to providing small firms with a larger slice of the federal pie? Small Business Administration lending programs are being curtailed, yet at the same time giant corporations are receiving government subsidies and are protected against failure. Continental Illinois, Conrail, Lockheed, and Chrysler are cases in point.

According to figures released by the Federal Procurement Data Center, in fiscal year 1982 small firms received only 4.8 percent of expended federal research and development funds as compared to 6.8 percent in 1980. Most of the funds went to a few giant companies. Yet, small firms have an innovation and invention rate at least 2 to 24 times greater per R&D dollar spent than large businesses, states the National Sciences Foundation. Berkley Bedell, a congressman active in small business affairs, suggested in a *Wall Street Journal* article that "to concentrate our research and development efforts among the large, centralized institutions virtually assures that we will be dependent upon those who have the greatest stake in maintaining the status quo." Most recently, small business groups have been waging a war to move a larger portion of the R&D funds in the direction of small firms. It is no secret that the big business lobby is fighting a ruthless battle to prevent this shift.

Even the current tax system favors big business over small. *Venture* magazine reports that federal income tax payments for *Fortune* 100 companies decreased from 18.6 percent in 1981 to 15.1 percent in 1983 while increasing for small firms from 22.9 percent to 28.7 percent during the same period.

In a country that prides itself on the effective utilization of limited resources, one would think that our system would promote and provide incentives to those institutions that have the greatest positive impact on society. Since the promulgated economic objective of our government is to foster full employment, it seems only logical to give those institutions that can satisfy this goal the adequate tools with which to do it more effectively.

The evidence indicates that the governmental process has a problem setting priorities, or maybe it is being influenced by well-financed special interest groups, as many have suggested, including President Reagan. This point can be illustrated by observing the recent attempts to rewrite or eliminate Section 7 of the Clayton Act, which prohibits the formation of monopolies. It also restricts mergers and acquisitions that significantly lessen competition within a specific industry. The government argues that this modification should be made because in Japan monopolistic companies and trading firms have been highly successful in penetrating foreign markets. The logic implies that "economics of scales"—in other words, "doing things in a big way"—provides for a more efficient means of applying resources. The bureaucrats reason that if the Japanese can do it, so can we.

Here we are again trying to apply foreign solutions to problems that are unique to the United States. Our difficulties can be directly linked to three factors. They have contributed to the primary economic problem of our day, which is industrial disintegration. Granted, it is not easy to admit one's shortcomings and even harder to take the medicine, but the difficulties exist and must be rectified. High wages, punitive tax laws, and ineffective managerial structures are the primary factors leading to the deterioration of our international and domestic markets. History has shown us that monopolies only aggravate these problems and do not solve them.

Changing Section 7 of the Clayton Act will augment our competitive difficulties and may signal the beginning of the end of the small business community. More and more assets are already falling into fewer hands. This will only accelerate the process, thereby allowing inefficient monopolies to dominate the economic landscape of America. Economic freedoms will be compromised and eventually personal liberty will be affected across a broad scale.

Misguided experts have chosen to present solutions that are less politically painful. The remedies that are officially recognized are only cosmetic in nature and effect. For example, it wasn't too long ago that many people were running around proclaiming that the high value of the U. S. dollar on international currency markets, relative to the currencies of other nations, was the major reason accounting for America's lack of competitiveness in world markets.* Undoubtedly, there is some truth to this notion, but let's not forget history either. During most of the 1970s the U. S. dollar was hitting historic lows compared to other world currencies, and at the same time our position in world trade shrank approximately 50 percent. Even more recently, the dollar has lost 30 percent of its value compared to other currencies, yet the country's trade imbalance has hardly improved.

A revamping of Section 7 of the Clayton Act will not solve our economic problems. Unfortunately, there are those who seem to be blurring the real issues at hand and trying to lead us into a future dominated by large monopolistic firms.

It would do us good to remember the embodiment of Section 202 of Public Law 163 which states:

> The essence of the American economic system of private enterprise is free competition. Only through full and free competition can free markets, free entry into business, and opportunities for the expression and growth of personal initiative and individual judgment be assured. The preservation and expansion of such competition is basic not only to the economic well-being but to the security of this Nation. Such security and well-being cannot be realized unless the actual and potential capacity of small business is encouraged and developed.

President Jimmy Carter hit the nail on the head when he stated:

> The small business community constitutes the single most important segment of our free enterprise system. It accounts for forty-eight percent of our gross national product, more than half of the American labor force, and continues to be the major source of inventions and new jobs. Small business is truly the backbone of the American economy.

Despite the enormous odds it faces, the emerging small business movement is taking its case to Washington and the state capitols with impressive flair and flamboyance. Lawmakers are beginning to get the message loud and clear, with some favorable legislation falling into the laps of small firms. With constituents at home screaming for more

*When the value of a country's currency is high relative to currencies of other nations, its exports will suffer, generally causing a negative balance of trade (imports exceeding exports).

jobs, and the primary job machine being small enterprise, you can bet that politicians will begin to court the entrepreneur.

A decade ago the catchword was "big is better." Today, nothing is farther from the truth.

Contents

"It's in your dreams, your aspirations that our future will be molded and shaped. You're the pioneers in America's continuing best and endless frontier—the free enterprise system."

"The greatest innovations for new jobs, technologies and economic vigor today come from a small but growing circle of heroes—the small business people, American entrepreneurs, the men and women of faith, intellect and daring who take great risks to invest in and invent our future.... You, too, can help us unlock the doors to a golden future. You, too, can become leaders in this great new era of progress—The Age of the Entrepreneur."

—PRESIDENT RONALD REAGAN

Chapter I

The Essence of Entrepreneurial Success

Characteristics of an Entrepreneur

Entrepreneurs seem to have common traits that account for their particular style of problem identification, problem solving, and creative endeavor, according to research studies conducted by the Small Business Administration and several think tanks. This is not to say that individual entrepreneurs must have every characteristic mentioned in the following pages, but most can claim to possess in one form or another a majority of those mentioned. Entrepreneurs experiencing gaps will fill the deficiencies, if possible, with subordinates or professionals possessing the skills needed to compensate for their weaknesses. This may also serve to complement the existing entrepreneurial team within a small firm.

The characteristics mentioned below will serve only as broad explanations. These behavioral traits will be observed and dissected in more detail as the book progresses.

AGE

Today, entrepreneurship generally knows no age limit. *Venture* and *Inc.* magazines consistently report on new businesses being pioneered by people ranging in ages from the late teens to the late sixties and in some cases even older. But there seems to be a higher concentration of entrepreneurial activity in the early thirties age class, according to the

Center for Entrepreneurial Management (CEM). Table 1 provides further evidence that most people tend to gravitate toward entrepreneurship between the late twenties and late thirties.

In all probability the medium age for entrepreneurship will tend to increase as the bulk of the baby boom generation moves through the life cycle. There are a lot of people falling within the ranks of this age group and they are all competing for limited employment opportunities. For example, *Venture* magazine reports that during this decade mid-level managerial jobs will rise by only 19.1 percent while the number of people between the ages of 35 and 44 will increase by 42 percent. Many frustrated baby boomers will opt for self-employment as a way to fulfill their personal and financial aspirations. Over the next couple of decades they will be experimenting with entrepreneurship on a large scale.

Herein lies a problem of societal proportion. People in large numbers will be using personal resources to start new enterprises later in life. Unfortunately, this is a time when they should be positioning themselves for retirement, especially in light of the uncertainty surrounding the Social Security system. Many experts agree that you

TABLE 1

AGE STARTING BUSINESS

Source: Copyright © 1981, National Federation of Independent Business Research and Education Foundation. Reprinted with permission from the "Small Business in America" poster.

should undertake entrepreneuring while you are still young enough to recover from losses if failure should occur. Waiting too long before taking the plunge can be risky in terms of future financial security.

Ascendency and Ego

Successful entrepreneurs govern and control wisely without excessive ego involvement. Studies show that they realize the importance of ego in obtaining goals, but they are also acutely sensitive to the negative impact of unrestrained ego and self-satisfaction. One New York venture capitalist who was interviewed for this book stated, "Restrained ego is a good quality to have when running a small enterprise, but the uncontrolled ego is dangerous and we will not commit funds to individuals displaying such behavior."

Anti-Organizational Outlook

Without a doubt, most entrepreneurs are not structured by nature and have an ingrained suspicion of formal organizational and authority systems. Even though they acknowledge the role of structure in the organization, they truly believe that structure is only superficial and that "informal systems" are the real guiding lights. One day while working on a consulting project at Techno Company, Inc., located in northern Virginia, Silvester & Associates was developing formalized procedures to measure profits and losses, productivity, and a variety of other factors. Bob Cain, Techno's president, complained that he despised formal procedures and organization. He acknowledged that his company had grown to the point where it needed some structure, but he was clearly upset about it. Mr. Cain was simply reacting like many other successful entrepreneurs experiencing organizational growth. For years they have been managing by the seat of their pants only to find that their companies have grown to the point where some structure is needed.

Most entrepreneurs generally feel that autocratic managerial systems are repugnant, but at times these same entrepreneurs display dictatorial tendencies. In reality, they prefer participative management, but they also understand its limitations, especially as it relates to small business enterprise.

THINKING CAPABILITY

Entrepreneurs are original and creative thinkers who have the ability to create new ideas and approaches in addition to thinking in unorthodox ways. They have a keen ability to make intelligent comparisons, and most can reason in practical, theoretical, and abstract terms. Entrepreneurs also have the knack of seeing the "bigger picture" as it relates to organizational goals, as opposed to typical corporate managers who generally have a segmented and parochial viewpoint. "Entrepreneurs must think or sink," according to one CPA who was interviewed for this book. Individuals unable or unwilling to think through the entire entrepreneurial process as it relates to their venture have no business risking time and financial resources. The business plan is the ultimate tool that forces prospective entrepreneurs to think. Poorly constructed business plans are normally not funded by capital outlets. More on this subject will come later.

COMMUNICATION ABILITY

Successful entrepreneurs generally communicate orally and in written format in a clear, concise, and logical way. They also have the ability to listen, absorb, and understand what other people are communicating. Several years ago a venture capitalist associated with Citicorp said, "If an entrepreneur cannot communicate the attributes of his product or service to me, how is he going to sell it to his customers? He's not worth the gamble." In addition, many of the entrepreneurs interviewed for this book indicated the importance of being able and willing to communicate with customers and employees.

CONNECTIONS AND CONTACTS

On one hot and sticky summer evening several years ago I was being interviewed on the Fred Fiske call-in radio show on WAMU in Washington, D.C. The topic was entrepreneurial characteristics, and a person called in identifying himself as a very successful entrepreneur. After his identification he opened a frontal attack on all business book authors for "not telling the truth" about entrepreneurship. He contended that entrepreneurial success is contingent upon only one factor—a person's connections and contacts. The caller vigorously argued that other elements made no difference. He said that he did not have any of the entrepreneurial characteristics mentioned that night, but his money contacts made him successful. Without a doubt, unlimited financial backing and/or access to free management expertise can turn anybody into a successful entrepreneur. Unfortunately, most people pursuing entrepreneurship are not that lucky and have to rely mostly on something less than sugar-daddies to ensure their success.

Connections, contacts, and networks will play an important role in helping you achieve entrepreneurial success. Making friends and establishing links with customers, funding outlets, suppliers, etc., will shorten the lead time associated with making the jump to entrepreneurship and does increase your chance of survival and success.

CONSTRUCTIVE HATE

True entrepreneurs have an ingrained hate of working for somebody else. When working for others, they are generally loners and their aggressive natures earn them the title of "boat-rockers." Many are ignored, discouraged, suppressed, and even viewed as rabble-rousers. Some have been pigeonholed rather than promoted. Others are driven from their companies and then go on to pursue entrepreneurship. Many leave of their own volition. According to the Center for Entrepreneurial Management, one thing is clear; the true entrepreneur goes to work "ready to be fired."

In addition, you will find that many existing and prospective entrepreneurs hate to lose. Failure is repugnant to them. They exist to win. This is not to say that they are insulated from failure. Certainly not. Many successful entrepreneurs first had to lose before winning. They will tolerate this failure as long as they believe it is part of the learning process that will ultimately lead them to success. Jack Nicklaus, world champion golfer and successful entrepreneur, sums it up by saying, "Before you learn to win, you have to learn to lose."

DRIVE AND MOTIVATION

Entrepreneurs tend to accept responsibility without hesitation. They are hard driving and want to see things finalized, and will take charge when necessary. Many are aggressive and will be the first to initiate action. Their motives are based on both monetary and psychological considerations, with a definite slant toward psychological satisfaction.

Also, entrepreneurs usually display limitless vigor and vitality, which probably accounts for their reputation as work enthusiasts and their willingness to work an average of 15 hours per day for many years before hitting it big. Other not-so-attractive motivational factors, such as guilt and sex, are discussed in another section of this chapter and later in the book.

EDUCATION

In past years it was common for many successful entrepreneurs not to have progressed educationally beyond the eighth grade. Even today the entrepreneurial landscape is littered with self-made, uneducated individuals. But a different trend is developing to suggest that gone are the days of the untamed and less-than-well-educated entrepreneur. We all know some dumb-acting "down home" country folk that could negotiate the shirt off your back while smiling and chewing Beech-Nut tobacco. But an ever-increasing number of prospective entrepreneurs possess bachelors degrees. In fact about 35 percent of new business starts are begun by individuals with four years of college or more and this percentage is growing.

This development should not discourage you from taking the plunge if you are something less than well-educated. On the other hand, you must realize that an increasingly complex business environment will call for more sophisticated credentials. Your ability to succeed will, in part, be contingent upon your willingness to seek out and employ professional assistance to fill the gaps left by your lack of knowledge.

EXPERTISE

Successful entrepreneurs tend to be experts in their fields, be they technical, operational, or administrative in nature. In fact, many entrepreneurs prior to becoming self-employed, either intentionally or unintentionally, assume intangible "power" roles with their employers based upon their accumulation of expertise. In addition, most small experts agree that a good knowledge of your product or service is one of the most important ingredients ensuring entrepreneurial success. Without it you're "like a ship without a rudder" and will surely hit the rocks.

FAMILY BACKGROUND

Your family background may provide an indication of whether you stand a good chance to be successful at entrepreneurship, according to the Center for Entrepreneurial Management (CEM). If you had a parent who was an entrepreneur, your probability of small business success is greatly enhanced. Enterprising moms and dads have a lot to contribute in molding the entrepreneurial spirit within their children. It's in the blood, so to speak.

Another interesting bit of data revealed by CEM is the fact that many successful entrepreneurs had parents or grandparents who were immigrants. Many immigrants, upon reaching the shores of America, were economically disadvantaged and unable to find jobs, which led them to self-employment. In addition, many had a heartfelt belief, even more than Americans, that the United States was the true "land of opportunity," and so they set out to lay their claim upon the fruits of its economic abundance. This belief has manifested itself in their children and grandchildren. Not so with people whose immigrant roots go further back than their grandparents. Somehow their background takes on a quality that leads to a dependence on the "Protestant work ethic" as a way to achieve economic and financial security. These people are conditioned from childhood not to take risks and to work for somebody else. They believe that if they work hard all their lives, the system will take care of them.

If your recent forebears were not immigrants and/or entrepreneurs—don't dismay. Just realize that America is still the greatest land of opportunity in the world and start unshackling yourself from the bonds imposed by the outdated Protestant work ethic. The road won't be easy. You may have to do battle with security-oriented spouses and barking mothers-in-law who are more interested in your collecting a regular paycheck than taking a risk at entrepreneurship. You may even have to fail a couple of times before achieving success.

GOAL ORIENTATION

Successful entrepreneurs are goal setters. They delineate strategies and develop well-defined tactics to accomplish their objectives. Most are task oriented, which allows them to segment goals into small parts.

The parts are examined, analyzed, and systematically conquered. Without this trait, entrepreneurial success would be impossible.

HUMANISM

Many entrepreneurs have rough edges and they can be difficult to deal with in a business setting. In part, this is due to their unique styles and their perceived self-made status. After achieving entrepreneurial success, many learn to blunt their offensiveness and seem to achieve a degree of maturity that gives them a sense of tactfulness. Most achieve the ability to get along with others in many different settings. They become empathetic and eventually appreciate the contributions of others.

FORTHRIGHT

Entrepreneurs are outspoken and in some cases downright rowdy. While employed by others, they are generally the first to point out project or organizational deficiencies. In many cases, they are also the first to provide remedial solutions to alleviate problems or reduce their impact on the organization. Their aggressive natures have earned them the title of boat-rockers. As mentioned before, many are ignored, discouraged, suppressed, and even viewed as rabble-rousers. Some have been pigeonholed rather than promoted. Many are driven from companies.

RISK TAKING

Entrepreneurs will give serious evaluation before committing time and resources to any project. They are not "dice rollers," as many have purported them to be. In fact, entrepreneurs will avoid taking big risks if possible benefits are not in proportion to the risks. Most classify themselves as "moderate risk-takers" and will only take calculated risks.

UNORTHODOX

Entrepreneurs are experimenters. They generally see the world quite differently than most corporate managers. Many of them realize the limitations of traditional problem-solving techniques, especially as they relate to modern and complex corporate dilemmas. To the entrepreneur, the Harvard Business School step approach to decision making is obsolete and even dangerous and they will search for new ways to deal with modern problems. For example, many entrepreneurs are adopting techniques that employ creative decision-making methods.

In essence, true entrepreneurs try to unshackle themselves from the traditional methods of decision making, even though most are conditioned to various techniques of problem resolution. Some have even adopted new thinking skills that will allow them to attack seemingly insurmountable and complex problems in new and unorthodox ways.

In summary, entrepreneurs are aggressive and they actively seek out and seize opportunities either by direction or by their own volition. Also, many are anti-organizational and are highly suspect of authority structures. Usually they approach the decision-making process in a less than traditional or unorthodox way. However, these factors are exactly what make entrepreneurs so vital to our society. Their undying efforts to introduce new products and processes, to explore new areas of endeavor, and to stimulate creative thinking have helped to reverse economic stagnation in this country.

Definition Is Really Impossible

Defining the term "perfect entrepreneur" may be as difficult as Jason's trek to find the golden fleece. Without a doubt, entrepreneurial characteristics will differ from one individual to another. For example, entrepreneurs from the corporate world who previously operated in a certain environment may be subject to a particular set of circumstances which could condition their behavior. To illustrate, some firms allow a large degree of entrepreneurial dynamics, which will obviously have a positive impact on creative endeavor. On the other hand, entrepreneurs finding themselves in restrictive employment environments will develop informal organizational systems designed to crack or circumvent formal barriers to entrepreneurial activity. Unfortunately, a lot of excess creative energy must be spent and/or lost in order to accommodate the restrictive internal environment. Each of these scenarios will condition behavior differently.

The individual company has a distinct "personality," as does the individual. That personality will determine to a great extent the development of entrepreneurial behavior. Given these distinct idiosyncrasies, it is dangerous to view entrepreneurs as generic animals with absolute common characteristics.

The Imperfect Model

Contrary to their purported image of "white knights," many entrepreneurs appear to have had or currently possess common character flaws. Some management experts contend that these imperfections would preclude any individual from obtaining the status of "economic savior." Not so. In fact, many of these flaws account for their tremendous drive to "make things happen," according to noted venture capitalist A. David Silver, who authored the book entitled, *The Entrepreneurial Life: How to Go For and Get It.*

Silver's research suggests that these creative entrepreneurial individuals had unhappy childhoods and were subjected to educational arrest. Some were social outcasts, small in physical build, and sickly in nature. Most were members of the lower middle and lower income classes. Thomas J. Stanley, the author of the National Affluent Study, backs up Silver's research by noting in a UPI interview that many successful entrepreneurs tended to have "deprived childhoods." Stanley also said, "Adversity is a better trainer and disciplinarian than anything else." These early misfortunes really provided the stage on which they learned the art of creative hurdle jumping.

Silver has suggested that as adults, many entrepreneurs seem to be driven by "guilt." Guilt derived from marriage, especially as it relates to divorce, seems to be a highly motivating force. Also many entrepreneurs tend to be "dominated" by their "mothers" and also have "extraordinary sex drives," says Silver. This may account for their unusual aggressiveness.

Despite their many personal flaws, which are in fact positive factors that have contributed to their entrepreneurial dynamism, true entrepreneurs can recognize and take advantage of personal inadequacies and convert these weaknesses into positive motivating forces.

There's More

Now I would hate to suggest that you have to be a sex-crazed devil to succeed in the world of entrepreneurship. Of course, this notion is absolutely silly, as is the belief that one must have a particular set of characteristics to be a successful entrepreneur. Obviously, the entrepreneurial landscape is filled with people possessing many different negative and positive attributes. William B. Gartner, a professor with the University of Virginia, hits the nail on the head when he suggests in a newspaper article that there exist many more differences among entrepreneurs themselves than between entrepreneurs and non-entrepreneurs. "The amount of variation is awesome," Gartner states. He goes on to say, "It's much more than between entrepreneurs and managers or between entrepreneurs and housewives. There are no special characteristics distinguishing the person who starts a business from the person who never does." He bases his comments on in-depth interviews with 300 founders of small- and large-scale businesses.

Gartner is encouraging in his findings by suggesting, "Anybody can learn to be a good entrepreneur.... Entrepreneurship is a learned behavior in the same way that tap dancing is. If a person spends time learning the tap dance process, he's probably going to become an okay tap dancer." He goes on to say, "People should never think of themselves as not having the potential to be entrepreneurs."

In a *New York Times* article, Howard H. Stevenson, a professor of entrepreneurial management at the Harvard Business School, states, "The role models show you don't have to be super flamboyant, super aggressive and totally confident person to be an entrepreneur. These [entrepreneurs] aren't superstars ... "

Gartner and Stevenson are right in their approach. Anybody can become a successful entrepreneur; however, for most of us it is a learning process. A few individuals are born with natural entrepreneurial instincts, but for the greater majority this simply is not the case. We do know that certain qualities are necessary to ensure entrepreneurial success. If these qualities are lacking, then they must be sought out through the learning process and instilled as a way of doing business. This chapter has discussed most of these qualities in a brief manner. The remainder of the book will dedicate itself to a more extensive examination.

Chapter II

Testing Your Way to Success

Take the Test Before the Plunge

One of the hallmarks of a successful company, be it small or large, is its unwillingness to commit large sums of money to the marketing of a product or service without first testing in a localized environment. In fact, companies will go to great pains and expense to extensively test a new product or service in a test environment in order to ensure that some degree of profit success can be expected if large sums of money are spent on a national marketing campaign. Without a test this determination would not be possible, thus exposing a firm to severe and potentially fatal losses in the event of a failed national rollout. Even if the testing shows that the product or service would fail in the marketplace, at least the company can withdraw from the market and only be at loss for the cost of testing.

Similar precautionary measures should be taken by individuals pursuing the dream of entrepreneurship. Unfortunately, too many people jump into self-employment without a clear understanding of the conditions that may be motivating them to action. Many fall prey to impulsiveness and fads generally leading to demise. Others forge ahead without a real understanding of what the future has in store. Many are just not suited to entrepreneurship because of such things as risk aversion, family background, strong sense of job security, etc. Whatever the case, it is extremely imperative that prospective and existing entrepreneurs have an idea about their chances of success before venturing too far. They must test themselves to ensure some possibility of entrepreneurial success before committing large amounts of time, money, and effort into an endeavor that may prove to be a psychological and financial disaster.

The Entrepreneur's Quiz*

Who are these people called entrepreneurs? Why do they seem more at home in a swivel chair than in an easy chair? What makes them lay their talent and skill on the line, not once, but over and over again? Why can't they just get a job? What's with them anyway?

Are they really smarter than most people? Do they know something that others don't? Or are they just crazy? Or maybe it's a combination of the three.

This entrepreneurial profile was developed from a series of questionnaire analyses performed by the Center for Entrepreneurial Management, Inc. (CEM). Founded in 1978, the Center is the world's largest non-profit association of entrepreneurial managers, with over 2500 members. It is headquartered in New York City.

Take the test now.

1. How were your parents employed?
   a. Both worked and were self-employed for most of their working lives.
   b. Both worked and were self-employed for some part of their working lives.
   c. One parent was self-employed for most of his or her working life.
   d. One parent was self-employed at some point in his or her working life.
   e. Neither parent was ever self-employed.
2. Have you ever been fired from a job?
   a. Yes, more than once.
   b. Yes, once.
   c. No.
3. Are you an immigrant, or were your parents or grandparents immigrants?
   a. I was born outside of the United States.
   b. One or both of my parents were born outside of the United States.

*This whole section was provided by permission of the Center for Entrepreneurial Management, Inc. (CEM).

   c. At least one of my grandparents was born outside of the United
      States.
   d. Does not apply.
4. Your work career has been:
   a. Primarily in small business (under 100 employees).
   b. Primarily in medium-sized business (100 to 500 employees).
   c. Primarily in big business (over 500 employees).
5. Did you operate any businesses before you were twenty?
   a. Many.
   b. A few.
   c. None.
6. What is your present age?
   a. 21-30.
   b. 31-40.
   c. 41-50.
   d. 51 or over.
7. You are the _____ child in the family.
   a. Oldest.
   b. Middle.
   c. Youngest.
   d. Other.
8. You are:
   a. Married.
   b. Divorced.
   c. Single.
9. Your highest level of formal education is:
   a. Some high school.
   b. High School diploma.
   c. Bachelor's degree.
   d. Master's degree.
   e. Doctor's degree.
10. What is your primary motivation in starting a business?
    a. To make money.
    b. I don't like working for someone else.
    c. To be famous.
    d. As an outlet for excess energy.
11. Your relationship to the parent who provided most of the family's
    income was:
    a. Strained.
    b. Comfortable.
    c. Competitive.
    d. Non-existent.

12. If you could choose between working hard and working smart, you would:
    a. Work hard.
    b. Work smart.
    c. Both.
13. On whom do you rely for critical management advice?
    a. Internal management teams.
    b. External management professionals.
    c. External financial professionals.
    d. No one except myself.
14. If you were at the racetrack, which of these would you bet on?
    a. The daily double—a chance to make a killing.
    b. A 10-to-1 shot.
    c. A 3-to-1 shot.
    d. The 2-to-1 favorite.
15. The only ingredient that is both necessary and sufficient for starting a business is:
    a. Money.
    b. Customers.
    c. An idea or product.
    d. Motivation and hard work.
16. If you were an advanced tennis player and had a chance to play a top pro like Jimmy Connors, you would:
    a. Turn it down because he could easily beat you.
    b. Accept the challenge, but not bet any money on it.
    c. Bet a week's pay that you would win.
    d. Get odds, bet a fortune, and try for an upset.
17. You tend to "fall in love" too quickly with:
    a. New product ideas.
    b. New employees.
    c. New manufacturing ideas.
    d. New financial plans.
    e. All of the above.
18. Which of the following personality types is best suited to be your right-hand person?
    a. Bright and energetic.
    b. Bright and lazy.
    d. Dumb and energetic.
19. You accomplish tasks better because:
    a. You are always on time.
    b. You are super-organized.
    c. You keep good records.

20. You hate to discuss:
    a. Problems involving employees.
    b. Signing expense accounts.
    c. New management practices.
    d. The future of the business.
21. Given a choice, you would prefer:
    a. Rolling dice with a 1-in-3 chance of winning.
    b. Working on a problem with a 1-in-3 chance of solving it in the allocated time.
22. If you could choose between the following competitive professions, it would be:
    a. Professional golf.
    b. Sales.
    c. Personnel counseling.
    d. Teaching.
23. If you had to choose between working with a partner who is a close friend, and working with a stranger who is an expert in your field, you would choose:
    a. The close friend.
    b. The expert.
24. You enjoy being with people:
    a. When you have something meaningful to do.
    b. When you can do something new and different.
    c. Even when you have nothing planned.
25. In business situations that demand action, clarifying who is in charge will help produce results.
    a. Agree.
    b. Agree, with reservations.
    c. Disagree.
26. In playing a competitive game, you are concerned with:
    a. How well you play.
    b. Winning or losing.
    c. Both of the above.
    d. Neither of the above.

Each answer in every question has a particular weight as indicated in the scoring profile below. Add up the weights of your answers to every question and write it down somewhere or hold it in your memory.

SCORING

1. a = 10
   b = 5
   c = 5
   d = 2
   e = 0

2. a = 10
   b = 7
   c = 0

3. a = 5
   b = 4
   c = 3
   d = 0

4. a = 10
   b = 5
   c = 0

5. a = 10
   b = 7
   c = 0

6. a = 8
   b = 10
   c = 5
   d = 2

7. a = 15
   b = 2
   c = 0
   d = 0

8. a = 10
   b = 2
   c = 2

9. a = 2
   b = 3
   c = 10
   d = 8
   e = 4

10. a = 0
    b = 15
    c = 0
    d = 0

11. a = 10
    b = 5
    c = 10
    d = 5

12. a = 0
    b = 5
    c = 10

13. a = 0
    b = 10
    c = 0
    d = 5

14. a = 0
    b = 2
    c = 10
    d = 3

15. a = 0
    b = 10
    c = 0
    d = 0

16. a = 0
    b = 10
    c = 3
    d = 0

17. a = 5
    b = 5
    c = 5
    d = 5
    e = 15

18. a = 2
    b = 10
    c = 0

19. a = 5
    b = 15
    c = 5

20. a = 8
    b = 10
    c = 0
    d = 0

21. a = 0
    b = 15

22. a = 3
    b = 10
    c = 0
    d = 0

23. a = 0
    b = 10

24. a = 3
    b = 3
    c = 10

25. a = 10
    b = 2
    c = 0

26. a = 8
    b = 10
    c = 15
    d = 0

This scoring is weighted to determine your entrepreneurial profile, the rating of which appears after the following analysis of the questions.

ANALYSIS

1. How were your parents employed?
    a. Both worked and were self-employed for most of their working lives.   4%
    b. Both worked and were self-employed for some part of their working lives.   10%
    c. One parent was self-employed for most of his or her working life.   36%
    d. One parent was self-employed at some point in his or her working life.   16%
    e. Neither parent was ever self-employed.   34%

1. The independent way of life is not so much genetic as it is learned, and the first school for any entrepreneur is the home. More than a third of our respondents came from homes where one parent had been self-employed for most of his or her working life, and two-thirds came from homes where a parent had tried to go it alone in business at least once.

2. Have you ever been fired from a job?
    a. Yes, more than once.   17%
    b. Yes, once.   34%
    c. No.   49%

2. This question is tricky because the independent-thinking entrepreneur will very often quit a job instead of waiting around to get fired. However, the dynamics of the situation are the same; the impasse results from the entrepreneur's brashness and his almost compulsive need to be right. Steven Jobs and Steven Wozniak went ahead with Apple Computer when their project was rejected by their respective employers, Atari and Hewlett-Packard. And when Thomas Watson was fired by National Cash Register in 1913, he joined up with the Computer-Tabulating-Recording Company and ran it until a month before his death in 1956. He also changed the company's name to IBM. The need to be right very often turns rejection into courage and courage into authority.

3.   Are you an immigrant, or were your parents or grand-
     parents immigrants?
     a.   I was born outside of the United States.   7%
     b.   One or both of my parents were born outside of the
          United States.   10%
     c.   At least one of my grandparents was born outside of
          the United States.   36%
     d.   Does not apply.   47%

3.   America is still the land of opportunity and a hotbed for
     entrepreneurship. The displaced people who arrive on our
     shores (and at our airports) every day, be they Cuban,
     Korean, or Vietnamese, can still turn hard work and
     enthusiasm into successful business enterprises. Our sur-
     veys have shown that, though it is far from a necessary
     ingredient for entrepreneurship, the need to succeed is
     often greater among those whose backgrounds contain an
     extra struggle to fit into society.

4.   Your work career has been:
     a.   Primarily in small business (under 100 employees)   62%
     b.   Primarily in medium-sized business (100-500
          employees)   15%
     c.   Primarily in big business (over 500 employees)   23%

4.   Small business management isn't just a scaled-down ver-
     sion of big business management. The skills needed to run
     a big business are quite different from those needed to
     orchestrate an entrepreneurial venture. While the profes-
     sional manager is skilled at protecting resources, the
     entrepreneurial manager is skilled at creating them. An
     entrepreneur is at his best when he can still control all
     aspects of his company. That's why so many successful
     entrepreneurs have been kicked out of the top spot when
     their companies outgrew their talents. Of course, that isn't
     always a tragedy. For many, it offers the opportunity (and
     the capital) to start all over again.

5.   Did you operate any businesses before you were twenty?
     a.   Many.   24%
     b.   A few.   49%
     c.   None.   27%

5. The enterprising adult first appears as the enterprising child. Coin and stamp collecting, mowing lawns, shoveling snow, promoting dances and rock concerts are all common examples of early business ventures. The paper route of today could be the Federal Express of tomorrow.

6. What is your present age?
    a. 21-30   18%
    b. 31-40   38%
    c. 41-50   26%
    d. 51 or over.   18%

6. The average age of entrepreneurs has been steadily shifting downward since the late 1950s and early 1960s, when it was found to be between 40 and 45. Our data puts the highest concentration of entrepreneurs in their thirties, but people like Jobs and Wozniak of Apple Computer, Ed DeCastro and Herb Richman of Data General, and Fred Smith of Federal Express all got their businesses off the ground while they were still in their twenties. We look for the average age to stabilize right around 30.

7. You are the _____ child in the family.
    a. Oldest.   59%
    b. Middle.   19%
    c. Youngest.   19%
    d. Other.   3%

7. There is no doubt about this answer. All studies agree that entrepreneurs are most commonly the oldest children in their families. With an average of 2.5 children per American family, the chances of being a first child are about 40%. However, entrepreneurs tend to be oldest children nearly 60% of the time.

8. You are:
    a. Married.   76%
    b. Divorced.   14%
    c. Single.   10%

8. Our research concluded that the vast majority of entrepreneurs are married. But then, most men in their 30s are married, so this alone is not a significant finding. However, follow-up studies showed that most successful entrepreneurs have exceptionally supportive wives. (While our results did not provide conclusive results on female

entrepreneurs, we suspect that their husbands would have to be doubly supportive.) A supportive mate provides the love and stability necessary to balance the insecurity and stress of the job. A strained marriage, the pressures of divorce, or a strained love life will simply add too much pressure to an already strained business life.

9.   Your highest level of formal education is:
      a.   Some high school.   1%
      b.   High School diploma.   17%
      c.   Bachelor's degree.   43%
      d.   Master's degree.   30%
      e.   Doctor's degree.   9%

9.   The question of formal education among entrepreneurs has always been controversial. Studies in the 1950s and 1960s showed that many entrepreneurs had failed to finish high school, let alone college. W. Clement Stone is the classic example. And Polaroid's founder, Edwin Land, has long typified the "entrepreneur in a hurry" who dropped out of college to get his business off the ground. However, our data concludes that the most common educational level achieved by entrepreneurs is the bachelor's degree, and the trend seems headed toward the MBA. Just the same, few entrepreneurs have the time or the patience to earn a doctorate. Notable exceptions include Robert Noyce and Gordon Moore of Intel, An Wang of Wang Laboratories, and Robert Collings of Data Terminal Systems.

10.   What is your primary motivation in starting a business?
      a.   To make money.   34%
      b.   I don't like working for someone else.   56%
      c.   To be famous.   4%
      d.   As an outlet for excess energy.   6%

10.   The answer here is pretty conclusive. Entrepreneurs don't like working for anyone but themselves. While money is always a consideration, there are easier ways to make money than by going it alone. More often than not, money is a byproduct (albeit a welcome one) of an entrepreneur's motivation rather than the motivation itself.

11.   Your relationship to the parent who provided most of the family's income was:
      a.   Strained.   29%
      b.   Comfortable.   53%

    c. Competitive.   9%
    d. Non-existent.   9%

11. These results really surprised us because past studies, including our own, have always emphasized the strained or competitive relationship between the entrepreneur and the income-producing parent (usually the father). The entrepreneur has traditionally been out to "pick up the pieces" for the family, or to "show the old man," while at the same time always seeking his grudging praise. However, our latest results show that half of the entrepreneurs we questioned had what they considered comfortable relationships with the income-producing parent. How do we explain this shift? To a large extent, we think it's directly related to the changing ages and educational backgrounds of the new entrepreneurs. The new entrepreneurs are children of the fifties and sixties, not children of the Depression. In most cases they've been afforded the luxury of a college education, not forced to drop out of high school to help support the family. We think that the entrepreneur's innate independence has not come into such dramatic conflict with the father as it might have in the past. We still feel that a strained or competitive relationship best fits the entrepreneurial profile, though the nature of this relationship is no longer so black and white.

12. If you could choose between working hard and working smart, you would:
    a. Work hard.   0%
    b. Work smart.   47%
    c. Both.   53%

12. The difference between the hard worker and the smart worker is the difference between the hired hand and the boss. What's more, the entrepreneur usually enjoys what he's doing so much that he rarely notices how hard he's really working.

13. On whom do you rely for critical management advice?
    a. Internal management teams.   13%
    b. External management professionals.   43%
    c. External financial professionals.   15%
    d. No one except myself.   29%

13. Entrepreneurs seldom rely on internal people for major policy decisions because employees very often have pet

projects to protect or personal axes to grind. What's more, internal management people will seldom offer conflicting opinions in big decisions, and in the end the entrepreneur makes the decision on his own.

Outside financial sources are also infrequent sounding boards when it comes to big decisions because they simply lack the imagination that characterizes most entrepreneurs. The most noble ambition of most bankers and accountants is to maintain the status quo.

When it comes to really critical decisions, entrepreneurs most often rely on outside management consultants and other entrepreneurs. In fact, our follow-up work has shown that outside management professionals have played a role in *every* successful business we've studied, which wasn't the case when it came to unsuccessful ventures.

14. If you were at the racetrack, which of these would you bet on?

a.	The daily double—a chance to make a killing.	22%
b.	A 10-to-1 shot.	23%
c.	A 3-to-1 shot.	40%
d.	The 2-to-1 favorite.	15%

14. Contrary to popular belief, entrepreneurs are not high risk takers. They tend to set realistic and achievable goals. While they do take risks, these are usually calculated risks. They know their limits, but are willing to bet on their skills. For instance, they'll seldom buy lottery tickets or bet on spectator sports, but they are not reluctant to gamble on games involving their own skill such as tennis or golf.

15. The only ingredient that is both necessary and sufficient for starting a business is:

a.	Money.	3%
b.	Customers.	44%
c.	An idea or product.	25%
d.	Motivation and hard work.	28%

15. All businesses begin with orders and orders can only come from customers. You might think you're in business when you've developed a prototype, or after you've raised capital, but bankers and venture capitalists only buy potential. It takes customers to buy a product.

16. If you were an advanced tennis player and had a chance to play a top pro like Jimmy Connors, you would:

a. Turn it down because he could easily beat you.   4%
b. Accept the challenge, but not bet any money on it.   78%
c. Bet a week's pay that you would win.   14%
d. Get odds, bet a fortune, and try for an upset.   4%

16. This question narrows the focus on the risk-taking concept and the results emphasize what we have already stated: entrepreneurs are not high rollers. What is interesting about this response is that more than three-quarters of our respondents would accept the challenge, not so much on the off-chance of winning, but for the experience, and experience is what entrepreneurs parlay into success.

17. You tend to "fall in love" too quickly with:
a. New product ideas.   40%
b. New employees.   10%
c. New manufacturing ideas.   4%
d. New financial plans.   13%
e. All of the above.   33%

17. One of the biggest weaknesses that entrepreneurs face is their tendency to "fall in love" too easily. They go wild over new employees, products, suppliers, machines, methods, and financial plans. Anything new excites them. But these "love affairs" usually don't last long; many of them are over almost as suddenly as they begin. The problem is that during these affairs, entrepreneurs can quite easily alienate their staffs, become stubborn about listening to opposing views, and lose their objectivity.

18. Which of the following personality types is best suited to be your right-hand person?
a. Bright and energetic.   81%
b. Bright and lazy.   19%
c. Dumb and energetic.   0%

18. The best answer isn't always the right answer. "Bright and energetic" is the best answer, but "bright and lazy" is the right answer. But why is that and why do entrepreneurs consistently answer this question incorrectly? Because the natural inclination is to choose "bright and energetic" because that describes a personality like your own. But stop and think a minute. You're the boss. Would you be happy, or for that matter efficient, as someone else's right-hand man? Probably not. And you don't want to hire an entrepreneur to do a hired-hand's job.

That's why the "bright and lazy" personality makes the best assistant. He's not out to prove himself, so he won't be butting heads with the entrepreneur at every turn. And while he's relieved at not having to make critical decisions, he's a whiz when it comes to implementing them. Why? Because, unlike the entrepreneur, he's good at delegating responsibilities. Getting other people to do the work for him is his specialty!

19. You accomplish tasks better because:
   a. You are always on time.   24%
   b. You are super organized.   46%
   c. You keep good records.   32%

19. Organization is the key to an entrepreneur's success. This is the fundamental principle on which all entrepreneurial ventures are based. Without it, no other principles matter. Organizational systems may differ, but you'll never find an entrepreneur who's without one. Some keep lists on their desks, always crossing things off from the top and adding to the bottom. Others use notecards, keeping a file in their jacket pockets. And still others will keep notes on scraps of paper, shuffling them from pocket to pocket in an elaborate filing and priority system. But it doesn't matter how you do it, just as long as it works.

20. You hate to discuss:
   a. Problems involving employees.   37%
   b. Signing expense accounts.   52%
   c. New management practices.   8%
   d. The future of the business.   3%

20. The only thing an entrepreneur likes less than discussing employee problems is discussing petty cash slips and expense accounts. Solving problems is what an entrepreneur does best, but problems involving employees seldom require his intervention, so discussing them is just an irritating distraction. Expense accounts are even worse. What an entrepreneur wants to know is how much his sales people are selling, not how much they're padding their expense accounts. Unless it's a matter of outright theft, the sales manager should be able to handle it.

21. Given a choice, you would prefer:
   a. Rolling dice with a 1-in-3 chance of winning.   8%
   b. Working on a problem with a 1-in-3 chance of solving it in the allocated time.   92%

21. Entrepreneurs are participants, not observers; players, not fans. And to be an entrepreneur is to be an optimist; to believe that with the right amount of time and the right amount of money you can do anything. Of course, chance plays a part in anyone's career—being in the right place at the right time; but entrepreneurs have a tendency to make their own chances.

22. If you could choose between the following competitive professions, it would be:
    a. Professional golf.   15%
    b. Sales.   56%
    c. Personnel counseling.   8%
    d. Teaching.   21%

22. Sales give instant feedback on your performance; it's the easiest job of all for measuring success. How does a personnel counselor or a teacher ever know if he's winning or losing? Entrepreneurs need immediate feedback and are always capable of adjusting their strategies in order to win.

23. If you had to choose between working with a partner who is a close friend and working with a stranger who is an expert in your field, you would choose:
    a. The close friend.   13%
    b. The expert.   87%

23. While friends are important, solving problems is clearly more important. Oftentimes the best thing an entrepreneur can do for a friendship is to spare it the extra strain of a working relationship.

24. You enjoy being with people:
    a. When you have something meaningful to do.   32%
    b. When you can do something new and different.   25%
    c. Even when you have nothing planned.   43%

24. Contrary to popular belief, entrepreneurs are not bores. They enjoy people and they enjoy being with people. They're extroverts—doers. To the entrepreneur there is no such thing as "nothing to do," so not having plans doesn't mean not having anything to do.

25. In business situations that demand action, clarifying who is in charge will help produce results.
    a. Agree.   66%
    b. Agree, with reservations.   27%
    c. Disagree.   7%

25. Everyone knows that a camel is a horse that was designed by a committee, and unless it's clear that one person is in charge, decisions are bound to suffer with a committee mentality.

26. In playing a competitive game, you are concerned with:
    a. How well you play. — 19%
    b. Winning or losing. — 10%
    c. Both of the above. — 66%
    d. Neither of the above. — 5%

27. Vince Lombardi is famous for saying, "Winning isn't everything, it's the only thing." But a lesser known quote of his is closer to the entrepreneur's philosophy. Looking back at a season, Lombardi was heard to remark, "We didn't lose any games last season, we just ran out of time twice."

    Entrepreneuring is a competitive game and an entrepreneur has to be prepared to run out of time occasionally. Walt Disney, Henry Ford, and Milton Hershey all experienced bankruptcy before experiencing success. The right answer to this question is *c,* but the best answer is the game itself.

YOUR ENTREPRENEURIAL PROFILE

235–285 .... Successful Entrepreneur*
200–234 .... Entrepreneur
185–199 .... Latent Entrepreneur
170–184 .... Potential Entrepreneur
155–169 .... Borderline Entrepreneur
Below 154 .... Hired Hand

*The average CEM member profile is 239.

You Be the Judge

As an academician for the past nine years, I have come to appreciate the fact that tests, in a general sense, are not that reliable in predicting anything. That is not to say that they are entirely useless. To the contrary, tests can prove to be helpful as subtle indicators of success or failure.

If you took the test in the previous section and did not measure up, don't give up your plans to pursue entrepreneurship, for heaven's sake. Many individuals would have failed this test miserably, yet they are very successful entrepreneurs. The secret to overcoming the odds against them was their willingness to candidly admit personal weaknesses, as they relate to entrepreneurship, and then to address the deficiencies in a meaningful way. Al Bolton, the owner of a regional trucking company in northwestern Virginia, sums it up by stating that when he needs help in business matters he simply "hires experts" to fill the void.

On the other hand, if after taking the test you really feel that you are not cut out for the entrepreneurial life, it is probably wise to follow your gut instincts. Bow out now before committing any more resources.

Chapter III

Taking the Plunge

Risks to Consider

Entrepreneurs love to take calculated risks. Some live for it. The concept of risk, as it relates to entrepreneurship, will be fully discussed in chapter fourteen. If you are thinking about a stab at entrepreneurship, you too will have to get used to the idea of taking risks. We have all heard the usual cliché that "riding in a car" or "walking across the street" is a risk, and without a doubt it is, but these risk encounters are in the normal course of human existence. The risks described below are what you will have to bear as an entrepreneur:

—Constantly Changing Buying Motives of Potential Customers— Rapid inflation and disinflation, compressed economic cycles, unanticipated trends, etc., can all have a significant impact on customer behavior, thus raising the threshold of risk.
—Number of Business Failures—The failure rate for small businesses is high.
—Possibility of Losing Money—Where you find potential reward the possibility of risk is always present. An individual can lose a considerable amount of money if the business is a losing proposition and he/she fails to bail out in time to cut large losses.
—Psychological Damage—Business failure can produce negative psychological effects that may haunt someone for a long time to come. Some will completely avoid a second try at self-employment.
—Long Hours—Contrary to popular belief, most successful en-

trepreneurs put in 12-hour days. Most work as hard as corporate executives and some even harder.

—Medium Income—Successful small business people make, on the average, about the same as a mid-level manager in a large corporation.

—Income Variation—Income derived from your own business will be less regular than that received from an employer's salary or wage. If you are starting a new business, the first six to twelve months might be difficult because the operation is normally functioning at a loss. Even after business income is generated, variations in profits can be expected because of many factors (seasonal business, slow accounts receivables, heavy inventories, etc.).

Rewards to Expect

A successful entrepreneur can expect various rewards that may be achieved in any number of ways. You have the obvious monetary rewards of earning your own living or maybe even becoming rich. On the other hand, non-monetary results seem to be of prime consideration to many entrepreneurs. The benefits you can expect from entrepreneurship are listed and explained below.

—Independence—Self-employment provides a degree of personal and economic freedom not found when working for somebody else.

—Economic Security—Many individuals feel that economic security can be gained through self-employment. Given the high level of employee cutbacks in large and medium-sized firms, sometimes self-employment becomes the only alternative. Some see it as insulation against future layoffs. Consequently, many business executives and hourly workers are seriously pursuing small business opportunities. More than a few are already running sideline businesses hoping to someday generate a full-time operation. Some studies have suggested that as many as 50 percent of American households are involved with entrepreneurship to some degree.

—Potential Profit—Where you find the potential for risk, profit opportunities also exist.

—Quality of Life—Many individuals find a high degree of fulfillment in self-employment. Some successful entrepreneurs have reported an enhanced self-image and positive attitude along with other psychological rewards.

—Good Economic Environment—With recession fears minimized and economic expansion underway, it is an ideal time to be starting a small business. This is even truer of service enterprises which comprise most of the nation's small firms. The service field is expected to be the fastest growing sector of the economy, accounting for 90 percent of the country's output by the turn of the century.

—Consumer and Business Confidence Is Up—Buyers and sellers are very positive about the country's economic prospects at this point. If it continues, economic growth will follow suit.

—Lower Inflationary Expectation—For the time being, inflation is under control and that is a positive note to investors, managers, and consumers. High inflation erodes confidence in the economy and recession normally follows in order to correct spiraling prices. Moderating wage awards, stable oil prices, and an inflation fighting Federal Reserve System should keep prices in check for the remainder of the decade.

—New Emphasis on Small Firms—Governments are starting to realize the importance of the small business sector to the whole economy. Consequently, more governmental resources and favorable tax legislation will be directed to the small business community. Someday in the near future the entrepreneur will be seen, not as an enemy to be wiped out, but as our economic salvation.

What to Ignore

Believe me, there are more bears on Wall Street than bulls, even in the best of times. Likewise, in life you generally come into association with more pessimists than optimists. People will inundate you with every reason in the world why not to start or buy a business.

Greg Simmons of Richmond, Virginia, is a prime example of a man who was caught in such a vise. He was an accountant working for his daddy's large CPA firm and stood a good chance of filling his father's shoes at some point in the future. Greg wanted to buy a small garage door sales and installation business. Well, when he announced his intentions to the world, fireworks went off. His wife and in-laws hit the roof. They wanted him to stay in a more "secure" and "stable" profession. Doesn't that sound familiar? Every reason in the world was cited why not to pursue this venture. Guess what—he bought the business and today is very successful and firmly self-employed. He is even diversifying into other areas. Unfortunately, his plunge into entrepreneurship was the spark that led to the end of his first marriage.

Many divorces are initiated due to "security conflicts"—spouses being insecure and unsupportive of the other entrepreneurial spouse, especially if the business enterprise succeeds in a big way. This problem will be further discussed in a later chapter.

The Wall Street Journal recently began an article with the following heading, "Bad Times May Be Best Time for Beginning a New Venture." Many small business experts believe, contrary to popular opinion, that the optimum time for starting or buying a business is in the middle of recession. This argument, which seems to defy common sense, says that during economic downturns resources such as labor, raw materials, and capital may be easier and cheaper to obtain. Generally, there is less competition for capital. In addition, many prospective customers will begin purchasing to build inventories or experimenting with new product or service ideas in anticipation of an economic upturn. Initiating business operations during a recession gives you the opportunity to be in the best position to take advantage of ensuing prosperity. Starting a business halfway through an upturn in the economy translates into lost revenue opportunities.

Our country is full of depressionites and doomsayers. The media is also permeated with those who are constantly predicting gloom and doom. Several weeks after Ronald Reagan was elected President in November 1980, Thomas "Tip" O'Neill, Speaker of the House of Representatives, declared the President's economic programs a failure. The statement was made months before Reagan's programs went into effect.

Even during periods of robust economic activity, we find people proclaiming that the "sky is about to fall." You can't afford to let these negative individuals sway you from your goals and aspirations. This is not to say that caution should be ignored. Obviously a period of positive economic growth is usually followed by a pause in the economy. If you plan for these in a meaningful way, their affects can be largely avoided.

John Palumbo, a very successful independent insurance agent in Northern Virginia, sums it up nicely by saying, "Hell, if I listen to everybody giving me reasons not to pursue self-employment, I would be working for somebody else."

Chapter IV

Disliking Your Employer

Hating Your Job Is the Key

Many research studies have shown that up to 80 percent of Americans are not satisfied in their current jobs. You are probably no exception. Working for someone else usually sets the stage for the 4-R's (redundancy, ritual, rot, and rut). Even mid-level corporate executives find themselves dealing with the 4-R's. However, managers on the gravy train (upper echelons of administration) may ignore them in favor of attractive salary and benefit arrangements.

Quite a few of the entrepreneurs that we interviewed for this book indicated an enthusiastic dislike of their employment situation prior to taking the entrepreneurial plunge. Al Bolton, the owner of a medium-size trucking company in Northwest Virginia, says, "One day while driving home I became angry at my boss. I began thinking that if my employer could be successful, then why not me. A friend of mine was losing his business and I bought one of his trucks. Everything else just seemed to fall into place." A few of the entrepreneurs studied were not so discomforted with the thought of working for somebody else, but they just wanted a challenge or the right to do "their own thing." Jonathan Smith, an owner of a Honda auto franchise, stated, "We want to reap what we sow and cultivate things to our liking."

Whatever the case, hating your job should not be your sole motivation for taking the plunge into entrepreneurship. After all, working for somebody else does offer some benefits that are hard to give up. For example, you get a regular paycheck and reasonable work hours. Personal capital is not a risk and you don't have to lose sleep over ups and downs in the economy. The general headaches associated with running a business are reserved for your boss. Conversely, working for another can make for some frustrating situations; in particular, when you have been bitten by the entrepreneurial bug.

Below is a listing and discussion of some complaints commonly voiced by individuals finding themselves working for others. Listen closely. You will notice that some apply to your situation. In addition, these conditions will become increasingly obvious as you approach the decision to opt for entrepreneurship.

BAD MANAGERS

The current managerial class is no longer capable of guiding the ship of competitive enterprise into the next decade or beyond, say some experts. Undoubtedly, many managers in this country appear to be suffering from a host of terminal diseases, including "creative atrophy" and "short-term" fever.

According to the Secretary of Commerce, Malcolm Baldridge, American management has become "too fat, dumb, and happy in the last 10 years" to compete in the international marketplace. "I don't think it's labor productivity that's a problem, I think it's management, and I speak as a former manager," the Secretary told a group of exporters several years ago. Professor Eugene Jennings, a management expert from Michigan State University, basically agrees with Baldridge's opinion, comparing the configuration of corporate management to a "light bulb" with few people at the top or bottom and bloated in the middle with "incompetents" and "mediocrities." Jennings implies that managers allowed this situation to occur because the heydays of the 1960s made it easy to pass on and justify the cost. Even though Robert Hayes of the Harvard Business School seems to be somewhat less intense about managerial demise, he does blame management for 50 percent or more of the problems facing business today, as he stated in a *U. S. News and World Report* article.

Unfortunately, the aforementioned evidence suggests that many corporate management structures are inflexible and unwilling to deal with the threats imposed by changing conditions. They refuse to heed the warning signals until it is too late. To illustrate, International Harvester paid its chairman of the board $1.4 million dollars per year to manage the company into ruin. Continental Illinois is another case in point, along with Lockheed. To change their managerial styles, even if it meant saving the company, represented a threat unto itself, so they continued to manage in the same old way which led to financial demise.

It is true. Many of our corporate institutions are permeated with managers who are ineffectual and stagnant, managers without focus or resolve. Most will not even take moderate risks, which are so vital to business growth and survival. Also, too many of today's managers place a premium on short-term benefits, often at the expense of long-term planning and effective utilization of scarce resources. Imitative pursuits rather than product development seems to be the name of the game nowadays. Even more startling is the fact that some of the brightest, most innovative, and motivated people in corporations have been ignored, discouraged, suppressed, and even viewed as boat-rockers. They have been locked-in rather than promoted. Many are driven from companies. Does this sound familiar?

Whatever the case, the American public has definitely lost faith in corporate executives. A Harris Poll has revealed that only 18 percent of those queried expressed a great confidence in American business executives compared to 29 percent in 1973 and 55 percent in the mid-1960s. The ugly products of this degenerative state of affairs can help explain why the once-revered American manager is now portrayed in other countries as a complacent fool lacking both focus and resolve.

BUDGETARY LIES

Many wage increases and bonus awards are based on budgetary considerations as opposed to revenue attainment. Obviously, you know that there is a close relationship between budgets and revenues, but don't be fooled by those lying numbers-crunchers who get their promotions based on what they can steal from you. How is this done? It is really simple. Most companies keep two sets of books. This is not to suggest wrongdoing on a broad scale. To the contrary, many firms must report their financial condition to stockholders, creditors, trade associations, etc., in accordance with accepted accounting principles. Sometimes these are referred to as "external books." In other words, specific accounting techniques must be employed in order to provide an accurate financial picture.

In addition, companies maintain a set of "internal books" that may or may not be a better reflection of financial condition. For example, in the late 1940s and early 1950s U. S. Steel Corporation argued that its internal accounting procedure was more accurate than its external procedure because it allowed, to some degree, for an accelerated write-off of assets. U. S. Steel executives argued that this was needed to counteract the effects of inflation on the replacement of equipment, because inadequate write-offs attributed to artificial profits. Taxes had to be paid on those profits, thus reducing cash flow and creating a disincentive for investment.

The point to ponder here is the fact that budgetary manipulations can paint almost any picture, although public and semi-private companies have some difficulty getting away with abuse. You saw what happened when the chairman of General Motors got a seven-million-dollar bonus after asking his workers to take wage and benefit reductions. This is not to say that internal budgets cannot be used as weapons against you. Obviously, they can, but it all comes out in the wash at the end of the fiscal year.

Smaller and medium-sized companies that are non-public or semi-public in nature are where most of the budgetary abuse occurs. For the most part, they are not required to conform to accepted accounting standards. The exception to this rule may occur when bankers and other creditors demand some reasonable form of accounting practices so as to make lending decisions, but they do not have to be according to accepted accounting principles.

To illustrate, a small savings and loan association located in West Virginia provided a yearly financial statement to its account holders and employees. Since this financial institution was a mutual organization, it did not have stockholders in a traditional sense. The account holders were the owners. Unfortunately, the financial statement only included a balance sheet (the statement of assets and liabilities). No income statement was provided. Federal laws did not mandate a reporting of income, except to the appropriate federal agency, of course. In 1977, the firm hired a young MBA with a finance major to train and run its first branch office. The young man wondered why income figures were not available. He used a simple technique to determine the profitability of his employer. He subtracted the "retained surplus," as reported on the previous year's balance sheet, from the "retained surplus" reported for the current year. The difference represented net income for the year not counting dividends paid to account holders.

Interestingly enough, the figures when compared to the savings and loan industry as a whole showed that this firm was the second most profitable savings and loan in the state on a proportionate basis and ranked fifteenth in the entire nation. Upon confronting the chief executive officer with these facts, the young man was told not to mention this to other employees. The CEO felt that if this information were known, the employees would demand more compensation than their current substandard wage. In other words, they were being deceived.

Another case involves a small college located in Northern Georgia and employing nearly 200 people. Since it is a private school it is not required to "make public" its financial statements. For years, the college paid its faculty a very low salary. In fact, it was the lowest-paid faculty in the state. In the spring of every year, when raises were announced for the next academic year, the college administration would harp on the college's sad state of financial affairs. Several militant faculty members breathed life into the college's faculty representation committee and started to negotiate with the school's administration about compensation. Faculty from the business administration department secured and analyzed the college's financial record going back ten years. Guess what? You got it. Over six million dollars in available funds were used to pay for constructing buildings over a period of a decade. Debt financing, for the most part, was not used because the college's administration knew that the faculty had traditionally been non-militant. So they reasoned that they could pay off the buildings using operating capital that should have been used, in part, to enhance already very low faculty salaries. Even after the discovery, the administration admitted to doing this, and it still does so today.

Another example worth noting deals with a case handled by the consulting firm of Silvester & Associates. A medium-sized manufacturing firm in Harrisonburg, Virginia, contracted this consulting organization to develop and implement managerial systems designed to enhance employee morale and productivity. The manufacturer was losing $13,000 per month. Silvester & Associates quickly acted by identifying profit and cost centers and then installing efficiencies where needed. Employee incentive systems were employed. The company started to make a lot of money, and so did the employees in the form of wages, benefits, and performance bonuses. Some of the bonuses accounted for up to 25 percent of wages. Productivity, profits, and morale all increased sharply.

About one year after completing the project, the consulting firm heard that their former client had gotten a little greedy and decided to manipulate budget figures in order to reduce bonuses. Upon buying new equipment in various departments, the company would expense the entire cost during the period in which bonuses were due to be paid, thus substantially reducing employee bonuses in that period. The original thinking upon setting up the incentive system was to expense new equipment over a number of years in order to reduce the cost impact on the various departments. In fact, this is how it is supposed to be done. Since the incentive program was based on quarterly profitability, bonuses declined and the manufacturer embarked upon replacing his equipment using current operating capital. The manufacturer complained that profits were low, but the workers quickly learned of his budget-fixing maneuvers and morale collapsed.

This brings to mind another case where a small but nationally known manufacturer of fine furniture decided to cut his employees' wages by 10 to 15 percent during the last recession. The week following the wage reduction the owner/operator bought a new $50,000 Mercedes-Benz. Now, you have to give the crook credit for being up front in the way he felt about the hired help.

BUREAUCRACY AND STYMIED CREATIVITY

Being an idea person and working for a large corporation can be a frustrating experience, to say the least. Large companies generally take on bureaucratic tendencies that can lead to organizational red tape, inaction, and inefficiencies. Obviously, some of this cannot be avoided. However, many corporate bureaucrats have gone to great length to ensure that new ideas and programs are never given quick consideration. In some cases, innovative projects that have been developed by bright employees are never reviewed.

Today, many corporate managers view decision-making as a precarious undertaking. Consequently, "passing the buck" and the avoidance of responsibility seem to be a popular exercise within corporate ranks. The bureaucratic organization provides the perfect environment for the "modern" and "weak-kneed" corporate executive who seeks to be protected from making even the smallest of decisions.

This is largely accomplished through "corporate review committees." By using a review committee to recommend a particular course of action, an executive can partially or fully remove himself/herself from the firing line if something goes wrong. To illustrate, a small private college purchased a computer and related software in the late 1970s to handle student accounts, grades, and other functions. After several years and nearly $300,000 in expenses, the college computer was very underutilized. Programs and records were in a shamble. Mistakes and gross inefficiencies were prevalent throughout the system. All of this culminated at about the same time that a new administration was taking over the reins of the college. The new president was appalled by the ineptitude associated with purchasing and running the college's computer system. Upon conducting an investigation to find the person responsible for purchasing this incompatible computer and software, it was discovered that a committee made most of the decisions and no one person could be held accountable.

Review committees can also be used to slow down, water down, revamp, redirect, modify, or eliminate any idea or project. Quite often a proposal will be "sent back for further modification" or tabled "pending additional review." In many cases the initial proposal never sees the light of day or is so revamped to everybody's liking that it is not quite the original idea that you had in mind. Does that strike a chord?

In addition, many shrewd bureaucrats use committees to expend human energies that might otherwise be used in a more positive way. Study and review committees having more than five members are useless. Research has shown that having too many committee members leads to a "pooling of ignorance" and aimless drifting in subject matter. Of course, this may be the objective of the committee organizer. Also, some experts have contended that corporate committees dominated or chaired by women are taken lightly by male counterparts. Many companies use them as window dressing. Keep in mind that women make up only 2.9 percent of the managerial ranks in this country.

If there is one thing that an entrepreneur can count on it is that inefficient bureaucracy will continue to act as a drag on corporate action. While new product ideas and innovations try to survive the time delays imposed by organizational committees, review procedures, and corporate bureaucrats, the entrepreneur can turn on a dime.

CAREER TRACKS AND PROMOTION POLICIES

Many companies will lock employees into career tracks that are both inflexible and hard to break. Most firms have a good idea of where they want a particular employee to be located within the organization ten years down the pike. This is especially true of large enterprises.

Unfortunately, structured career tracks and promotion policies can lead to frustration for those of you who are ready to move up but are prevented from doing so because some corporate bureaucrat says it's against the rules. In addition, the career track mentality could stop you from moving into another field within the same firm even if it is justified in terms of qualification and interest. Sometimes top management will use career tracks and structured promotion policies as ways to stymie the upward mobility of younger mid- and lower-level managerial personnel. Also, and quite often, promotions are granted based upon internal political considerations. These "beauty contests" are less than optimal from an organizational standpoint and can leave a bitter taste in the mouths of better qualified but non-promoted employees.

Now, let's not get the wrong idea here. Personnel needs assessment is a very important part of the total planning function within a company and any responsible board of directors would demand it. Very often this function takes on an inflexible quality which is translated into rigid promotion criteria. What is sad is the fact that some very productive employees are not promotable due to these rigid standards. Morale, productivity, and profitability suffer over the long run.

CORPORATE POLITICS

The great Greek philosopher Aristotle once stated, in so many words, that if society could remove politics from its institutions then mankind could move forward at a much more rapid rate.

It is well known by many that the injection of political considerations into the management problem-solving process will normally generate a less than optimum solution. Quite frequently the best alternative is set aside, because of internal corporate expediency, in favor of a less appropriate remedy. Consequently, resources are not allocated to their fullest. Obviously, this is a widespread practice throughout the American business culture. It will more than likely continue; although, the price of such actions will steadily rise as the marketplace toughens due to enhanced competitive pressures. For example, the Methodist Church has been declining in membership for many years. In the State of Virginia, it has receded 4 percent in one eight-year period. What is interesting is the fact that this deterioration has coincided with an increase in politics within the management structure of the Church. One disillusioned Methodist seminarian said, "The church places more emphasis on politics than it does on the worship of God." This political environment has affected church management on all levels. Political decision-making seems to reign supreme over optimal judgment, and it is having a negative impact on the health of the entire church. Other religious denominations also suffer from the same affliction.

The real tragedy concerning corporate politics is its effect on employee morale and productivity. You all know people who have been awarded promotions, salary increases, and bonuses because they were expert boot-lickers or friends of the boss. Unfortunately, many companies place a high premium on factors such as attending office parties and padding the "right" egos. They encourage these activities as ways to get ahead. Some astute, although worthless, employees have achieved a great deal of expertise in this field called "political positioning." To some degree it accounts for the famed "Peter Principle," where incompetent people can be promoted if they are noticed and in the right place at the right time. Of course, this lessens the opportunities for those of you who are productive and less inclined to toe the political line.

What else can you expect in these times when mass conformity, patronization, and boot-licking have been the primary keys to surviving in corporate America. A poll taken two years ago revealed the startling impact of "conformity management." Thousands of personnel managers from major companies across the country were asked to state and rank their hiring qualifications for new executives. First on the list for over 70 percent of managers polled was the ability of the prospective employee's personality to conform to the company's personality. Many companies are actively testing prospective employees to ensure a "personality match." In other words, in the eyes of the personnel managers, conformity was the most important consideration in choosing a new employee. So much for creativity. Technical capacity, or the ability to do the job, was rated fifth.

Walter Sonyi, a principal with the human resource consulting firm of Goodrich and Sherwood Company, was quoted by *Industry Week* magazine as suggesting that in the final analysis many executives are hired based on how their organizational and personal chemistry conform to company standards. He said that one CEO in charge of international operations stated that he "based his hiring decision in part on who would sit beside him on an eight-hour flight."

Now, don't fool yourself into thinking that corporate politics will disappear. Surely, external forces that mandate the more efficient use of resources will serve to restrict the injection of politics in the management decision-making function. Nevertheless, corporate "politiking" is an ingrained American business practice that is expected to be around, in one way or another, for some time to come.

INAPPROPRIATE COMPENSATION STRUCTURES

Many companies strive to establish rigid compensation structures which can have a negative impact on the morale of productive employees. A lot of these structures are not designed to deal with the exceptional or innovative employee who deserves a compensation package that is more favorable than the norm. For example, companies will establish "salary cells" for every classification of employee. Sometimes governmental regulations require such categorizing. Each cell contains a salary range. If a very productive employee is at the upper range of a particular salary cell, without the prospect of moving into a new cell via promotion, compensation increases will be limited. Increases will only be realized when the whole cell moves, as is the case with cost of living increases. Many bonus systems are set up on the same basis.

It is hard to understand why more companies do not make their compensation structures more flexible in order to accommodate bright and productive employees. Obviously, part of the problem has to do with rocking the boat. The mediocre employees, who are generally in the majority, would raise hell if certain employees, even if they are more productive, were to receive something they did not. This situation could lead to organizational disharmony. On the other hand, many of these innovative and hard working people will leave these other than thankful companies for higher paying employment only to be replaced by less productive employees. Generally speaking, and in more cases than not, these replacements are hired at higher salary levels than the former employees.

What did we say earlier about bad management?

INTERNAL EMPIRES

Empire building within many corporate organizations has reached epidemic proportions. Some managers will construct internal empires just for the sake of exercising power and extending authority, even if their operating units become inefficient and lack effectiveness. Many of these managers will even forsake profit if power can be substituted for loss profitability. An example of this can be seen in the dispute between a maverick entrepreneur and Disney Productions. The entrepreneur informed the Disney executives that he would purchase a controlling interest in the company on the open market. The offer was very favorable to the stockholder. The executives reacted by spending several hundred million dollars of the stockholders' money trying to block his purchase. In essence, they compromised profits in order to maintain control for themselves. Disney stockholders have sued the executives.

Empire building is very prevalent among managers with long military backgrounds and those individuals with substantial government experience. These managers were nurtured in an environment void of fiscal constraint and profit responsibility. Most commanded many layers of subordinates. They loved to give orders, and in some cases, orders were given for the hell of it without any purpose in mind. Many have carried their managerial styles with them to the corporate world.

Likewise, many managers who have been around for a while are prone to empire building. Most were integrated into corporate America during a period of undisturbed economic growth, low interest rates, protective tariffs, and rising standards of living.

LACK OF SECURITY

Once upon a time in America, you could graduate from college or high school and be assured of a decent job offering some degree of employment security. In decades past, college career counselors were telling their prospective grads to go out and find a comfortable job with a big company. The students were lectured that if they played the company game, they would be taken care of by the system, and to some extent that was true. Unfortunately, this approach has contributed to managerial demise in many industries. Because of domestic economic pressures, in particular historically high interest rates and international competition, more companies are forced to reevaluate the application of their resources. Obviously, since human labor is generally the largest resource at a company's disposal, it has come under extreme scrutiny. White- and blue-collar jobs have been eliminated by the millions. Many corporations have done away with various levels of management. General Motors is an example of such a company.

Many people who have been employed by the same company for years are being forced into early retirement. Some are terminated altogether. Marginal employees do not stand a chance. And all of this is happening even in the best of economic times. Ford Motor Company has announced its intention to reduce its white-collar workforce some 20 percent by 1990. And in 1983 Du Pont increased its profits over the previous year by 26 percent with 9000 fewer employees. These and other examples were mentioned earlier. This situation is happening throughout many industries, with terminated careers strewn across the battlefields of corporate America. The message is clear. Today, it is a mistake to depend entirely upon others for your livelihood.

MENTORING

Unfortunately, we live in a time that encourages acute boot-licking and mentor attachment as a way of getting ahead. Now, don't delude yourself. Mentors can exercise enormous power over their followers. In fact, mentors find themselves in their positions because they have achieved one or more power bases within a company. They use these bases as platforms to exert authority. Some power bases are tangible while others may be intangible. To illustrate, an individual may achieve direct (tangible) power from some upper level of management. Tangible power may permit an individual the authority to reward and/or impose punishment. On the other hand, indirect (intangible) power may be achieved because one possesses expert knowledge and/or charismatic features.

Even though mentors usually command substantial power and influence, don't succumb to the mentor syndrome. Srully Blotnick, a *Forbes* magazine columnist, surveyed five thousand managers and found that only 1 percent gave credit to mentors as a reason for success. Another study conducted by the National Sciences Foundation (NSF) indicated that having a mentor is a risky business. NSF tracked three thousand mentor/protegé relationships and found that only thirty-four pairs lasted more than three years without a dispute that terminated the affiliation. In addition, the study found that more than 40 percent of the protegés reported being terminated by their mentors. Indeed a startling find when you consider the number of experts and publications telling people they must find themselves mentors in order to succeed in their careers.

These points can be driven home more forcibly by getting a little more personal. Jane Hess, a business professor with a small college in North Carolina and former corporate executive states, "When my mentor was fired, I lost my power base and I was eventually forced to leave."

Unfortunately, mentoring is ingrained in the corporate culture of many companies. It seems to be a philosophical impairment unlikely to go away soon.

NEPOTISM

Nepotism is as old as work itself. And it will continue as long as the "good ole boy" network remains intact. Now, there are some firms that have tried to deal with nepotism through various screening processes and have met with success. However, the vast majority of companies are still plagued with it. Smaller firms seem more inclined to tolerate nepotism for obvious reasons. Many are family operated enterprises anyway. It is called the "Blood Is Thicker Than Water" syndrome. Even though you may be appalled by such activity, upon becoming an entrepreneur, you too may be lured or forced to accommodate nepotism as a way of life.

RISK AVERSION AND SHORT-TERM FEVER

The U. S. Department of Commerce has suggested that American companies have become "risk averse" and unwilling to speculate in new endeavors. Short-term payoffs are sought by imitative pursuits and mergers. They have replaced new product development as the main thrust into new markets. Obviously, competition and price levels suffer, not to mention the misallocation of corporate resources due to misguided short-term, though secure, profit opportunities. Con- sequently, bright and inventive employees with new and/or innovative ideas will often find their projects unacceptable within the corporate ranks unless they offer the possibility of immediate return. Experimentation is passé, so to speak.

Now, who do we blame for this sorry state of affairs? Well, it would be easy to point our fingers at the corporate executives. And they do share some of the blame. However, other factors enter into the equation. For a long period of time, government tax policies did not attempt to encourage adequate investment in new ideas, innovation, and other risky endeavors. To some extent, President Reagan's Economic Recovery Act of 1981 has corrected that situation. On the other hand, current tax policies continue to encourage stockholders' demands for immediate earnings from their corporate managers. As long as corporate salary increases, bonuses, and promotions are based on short-term operating results, managers will continue to manage for the short term without giving thought to long-term consideration. Therefore, many new ideas and products that may require large up-front investment, testing, and patience will never reach the market.

Throughout the 1960s and 1970s a large number of firms of all sizes shifted their corporate goals. Less risky and short-term objectives were pursued. During this period many firms started to state their corporate objectives in terms of "profitability" as opposed to "market share." For example, General Motors Corporation had as its corporate goal during this period a 20 percent return on investment—a short-term profitability objective. Unstable petroleum prices throughout the 1970s caused the American automobile market to bend in many different directions. Foreign auto producers, on the other hand, took a "market share" approach when penetrating the American market and achieved a dominant position due to their willingness to "stay the course" and to make the necessary up-front sacrifices. In pursuit of enduring profits, the American auto giants fell prey to the ever-vacillating car purchaser.

Some American companies are starting to see the light. Remington Corporation adopted a "market share" posture. They were willing to absorb price reductions and huge advertising expenditures in order to boost their share of the market. If successful they will substantially enhance their competitive position and probability of survival. Texas Instruments proved this while competing with the now defunct Bomar Corporation. Texas pursued long-term market share while Bomar lusted after immediate profits.

How many times does history have to repeat itself before the message is absorbed? Unfortunately, the lessons of the past are seldom remembered in the world of commerce.

Resent Your Way to Success

Intelligent comparison and analysis quickly shows that any "entrepreneurial-oriented" person would soon become very uncomfortable working in an environment encumbered by one or more of the conditions mentioned in the previous sections. It is your right to be ticked off at your employer for giving your promotion slot to some half-wit whose only claim to fame is skillful boot-licking. Likewise, feel free to dislike your boss for not following through with promises to pay bonuses and award adequate salary increases, especially when you have earned them. In addition, don't blame yourself for hating the boss who steals your ideas and then takes full credit for them if they are successfully applied. You can expect that same superior to point his finger at you if an idea goes haywire.

Now, don't feel alone. Millions of employees are faced with some of the same aforementioned situations. Unfortunately, these negative management characteristics are more the norm than the exception. This leads to a misallocation of the country's resources across a broad scale. Many experts, including Malcolm Baldridge, Secretary of the U. S. Department of Commerce, believe that bad management in the private sector is contributing to many of our long-term economic problems. Without a doubt, this state of affairs is partially responsible for the nation's inability to compete in world markets, thus contributing to our $150 billion trade deficit. It will ultimately affect our standard of living.

Where do you direct your anger? Well, if your boss fits the typical "managerial mold," most likely he/she is an organizational caretaker lacking in motivation and creativity. His/her main objective is to maintain the system and status-quo. You will even find this to exist in small firms. Refuse to tolerate this situation and kick up your heels. Tell your employer to take a hike. Strike out and take the plunge. Become an ENTREPRENEUR.

The Price Paid for Independence

Entrepreneurship can carry a heavy price tag. Earlier sections of this book have already shown you the risks associated with striking out on your own. In summation, embarking upon an entrepreneurial endeavor is a risky proposition providing, on the average, only a medium income potential accompanied by long working days. For every three businesses that are formed, two cease to exist and the battlefield of entrepreneurship is littered with the debris of broken marriages, lost money, and shattered self-concepts.

The Wall Street Journal recently reported that the Chicago consulting firm, Challenger, Gray & Christmas, tries to discourage some executives from pursuing entrepreneurship. The president of the firm states, "If they are over 50 years old and don't have good marketing skills, they're likely to fail." He also says, "Many executives don't realize that they will have to forego the status and staff that established companies provide." The article went on to report that a New York recruiting firm, Gilbert Tweed Associates, "gets resumés from former executives who tried going it alone but want corporate jobs again."

Even upon achieving entrepreneurial success, you will still need to answer to various societal and business elements that could potentially restrict your ability to freely run your business. These elements are:

—Government Agencies
—Creditors
—Customers
—Vendors
—Distributors and Dealers
—Critical Employees
—Partners or Stockholders (if incorporated)
—Board of Directors (if incorporated)
—Unionized Employees
—Trade Memberships
—Family

For example, creditors could impose certain restrictions on your assets as a condition for granting credit. Unionized employees could strike, and vendors may be late in providing needed raw materials, thus creating delivery delays culminating in lost customers. Distributor networks can break down or shift and the government can demand anything from you at a moment's notice. At this point let's not get into a discussion about the impact of the family on entrepreneurship. Suffice it to say that it is very substantial and at times a major source of contention.

Chapter V

Where Are You Going?

Set Your Goals Now

Not only do you need to have identifiable goals and objectives, but a plan of action is a definite must. Very few individuals have become successful entrepreneurs without knowing where they are going and how they are going to get there. If you are still working for somebody else, set a timetable for breaking away and taking the plunge. However, if you are currently an entrepreneur but lack goals and specific plans, now is the time to sit down and do some thinking.

Listed below are some common goals that you may consider. Please be advised that this is not a complete list by any stretch of the imagination. They are offered as a guide only. Great care should be taken when delineating one's own goals. Every individual situation is different and that in itself necessitates careful consideration and unique planning.

— I want to be self-employed within the next eighteen months.
— I would like to provide for all of my family's needs within two years.
— I want to be financially independent within ten years of starting my own business.
— I would like to employ my wife and/or children.
— I would like to pass on a viable business to my heirs.

Your goals should be so structured that there stands a reasonable chance of attainment. Goals that are unrealistic will only lead to frustration and nonfulfillment. In addition, keep them simple and to the point. Make sure they can be reviewed and evaluated as time progresses.

Once your goals have been visualized, the next step is to formulate various "plans of action" that will provide you a roadmap into the realm of entrepreneurship. "Action plans," as we will call them, are multi-purpose guides that will point you in the right directions. They are described below.

— Short-Term Plans—These plans are designed to lead to the successful culmination of goals that must be achieved within one year.
— Intermediate Term Plans—These plans provide a roadmap to the successful culmination of goals that must be achieved within one to five years.
— Long-Term Plans—These action plans are structured to help you culminate objectives that must be achieved in a timespan exceeding five years.
— Contingency Plans (also known as "Crisis Plans")—These action plans are "trigger" mechanisms designed to react in the event that one or more forces external to the enterprise threatens its existence. Fifteen years ago very few firms planned for the unanticipated. Economic and financial cycles were fairly predictable. The Arab oil embargo changed all that. Any American firm, large or small, is faced with many external forces, also known in management circles as "uncontrollables." These forces fall outside the direct control of managers and sometimes even the whole political process in this country. Table 2 lists some of these threats.

Planning is the most important part of the decision-making process. It shows the way—a beacon of light, so to speak. Planning is a must for larger firms. Likewise, smaller entrepreneurial enterprises ultimately must embrace planning in order to survive highly competitive environments. What must be remembered about planning is the fact that it is a dynamic process that must be reviewed and modified on a regular basis. A 20-year long-range plan that was developed in 1970 should not look the same as it did 15 years ago. If it does, you are in trouble.

This kind of inflexibility will lead to grave miscalculations in the marketplace. Look at electric utility companies that planned, in the

TABLE 2

ENVIRONMENTAL/EXTERNAL FACTORS

Economic Cycles
Business Trends
Government Regulations
State of Technology
Competitive Conditions
Changing Demand Patterns
Industry Trends
Unions
Inflation
Changes in Population Profile
International Events

Source: *How to Start, Finance and Operate Your Own Business,* published by Lyle Stuart, Inc.

mid- and late 1960s, to build atomic power plants without paying close attention to the small but growing anti-nuclear lobby. Since the early 1970s the lobby, whether you agree with them or not, has been very successful in halting or slowing the construction of many of these plants. In some cases, the profits of the utility companies have been adversely affected. Of course, as with any "natural" monopoly, the costs incurred due to poor management forecasting is normally passed on to the consumer in the form of government-sanctioned price increases. But the above illustration is only one example. Without flexibility in planning and proper reevaluation on a periodic basis any size company in any market could succumb to the same fate. And if the enterprise is not a government protected monopoly, the costs incurred may have to be absorbed in the form of lost profits, since consumers are becoming increasingly price conscious of late.

This whole discussion brings us to a point where the topic of "strategic planning" must be given some consideration. Even entrepreneurial firms must strive to understand the strategic implications of their markets. Strategic planning is not as difficult or intimidating a concept as many management textbooks would suggest. It is simply an evaluation of your product's or service's strengths and weaknesses as they relate to the external forces mentioned in Table 2. This evaluation should be an ongoing process taking place at least twice a year. Your planning strategies (short-term, intermediate-term, long-term, and contingency plans) should be adjusted to reflect the external forces. In other words, as the potential impact of the forces change, so should your planning strategies. For example, in light of recent events within the international oil industry, the OPEC nations are now divided and indecisive. Many experts contend that we may experience a reasonable period of stable and falling petroleum prices. Obviously, energy prices, which is an uncontrollable external force, is not as much a threat to the economy, or particular markets, as it was in the past. Your planning should reflect this fact until events necessitate a reevaluation.

Organize Yourself

Once you have identified your goals and have your "plans of action" in place, the next step is to organize the factors of production (land, labor, capital, and management). These factors make it possible to offer something, a product or service, to sell. They are interrelated. In other words, all four must exist simultaneously, or conducting business would not be possible. This does not mean that each of the factors carry the same weight of importance. To the contrary, each factor will carry a different degree of importance depending upon the particular situation. For example, firms that are equipment and/or labor intensive will demand large working capital requirements. On the other hand, service enterprises are generally small by nature, and the primary initial emphasis is placed on management.

The organizing function is where you separate the men from the boys. It's the point where you must commit financial resources.

Actualize Your Dreams

After your factors of productions are in place you are ready to roll. At this point you have invested a lot of time and money. Turning back now would be costly because nothing could be recovered short of any land or equipment that had been purchased. The decision to back out should have been made long ago in the planning stage. Now your battle cry should be, "The only thing to it is to do it."

Truth or Consequences

Once operations commence, there is a need to utilize "control" through the use of "feedback" procedures. Productivity, sales, profit, and quality control reports are but a few of the feedback mechanisms that can be employed to determine whether you are doing things right. It is not enough to just sit back and watch your entrepreneurial enterprise operate. An intricate part of management entails controlling, through feedback, to ensure effective operations. You may have the best product or service in the world, but to rely on that alone isn't enough. The sales of this product or service may not be generating sufficient profits, or imperfections may be too high. Whatever the case, continued and appropriate feedback control will inform you of these and other difficulties before large-scale damage is incurred.

As a management consultant and director of the Small Business Institute at Shenandoah College, I have advised and encountered hundreds of entrepreneurial enterprises throughout the years. It really amazes me to witness the number of these small firms that lack, almost completely, any control features. The first thing that I request to examine is their financial statements (balance sheet and income statement). These statements are the simplest forms of control mechanisms. In 90 percent of these cases I am given a checkbook and/or tax returns, which are the farthest thing from financial statements, and many of these are improperly balanced.

This brings to mind a two-million-dollar-a-year company that hired me as a turnaround consultant. They were suffering employee morale problems and losing $13,000 per month. Now, they did have financial statements, but they were flawed, along with their tax returns. To make matters worse, their incompetent accountant was charging them six times what a CPA would have charged to do it right. This company had four separate operating units. Upon asking for financial and operating data for each unit, I was shocked to discover that none existed. The president's face turned three shades of red and he explained to me that all the company's sales and expenses figures were lumped together into what he described as the "soup bowl."

My first move was to fire the current accountant and retrieve some of his unjustified fees. After this was successfully completed, I worked with the new CPA to establish each operating division as a separate profit/cost center. Organizational overhead costs were allocated to the various divisions according to their contribution to total sales. After reviewing historical data and operating under the new financial "control" system, we discovered that two of the divisions were consistently losing money.

A decision had to be made whether to eliminate the unprofitable divisions or to impose efficiencies in an effort to turn them around.

Employment was cut in the unprofitable divisions and also in the divisions that were making money, although not to the same degree. Remaining employees were expected to work harder. Incentives systems were installed to recirculate partial cost savings and the positive effects of higher production output back to the remaining employees. Guess what? Employee morale increased sharply along with productivity. Profit climbed to over $10,000 per month and in one month exceeded $30,000.

The point to remember here is that proper financial control made this turnaround possible. It is really sad to think of how long profits suffered due to the lack of "feedback management." A few simple procedures could have avoided the problems described above.

The Ultimate Plan

As a business journalist, management consultant, and college professor, I feel it is my duty to give entrepreneurs the best advice that my knowledge and experience can provide. In this regard, I am committed to providing in all of my teachings and writings a thorough description and discussion of the "business plan." My reasoning for this is simple and relates to the large number of entrepreneurial failures.

A business plan has been traditionally viewed as a document used in raising capital to start or expand a business endeavor. However, it does have another purpose which is largely ignored. The business plan is first and foremost a "planning" device. Its secondary function is to raise capital. The preparation of the plan forces its author and designer—the entrepreneur— to evaluate entirely the prospects for success or failure in the marketplace. Creation of a good business plan is a grueling process taking months to complete. The final plan, ranging anywhere between 30 and 100 pages in length, is the ultimate testimony as to whether your product or service will be successful in the marketplace. The process forces you to look at everything related to the business venture beginning at the present and extending five years into the future. Capital requirements, competition, and operational considerations are but a few things reviewed and dissected in the business plan.

Constructing a business plan is like taking out an insurance policy. It will minimize your risks. Whether you are just starting your entrepreneurial enterprise or already in operation, it is essential to develop a business plan. In the process, both opportunities and hazards will be identified. The plan may convince you not to pursue your venture any further, in which case, it has done you a favor. "Why throw money down a dry hole?" On the other hand, the business plan could verify the need for a particular product or service, but at the same time it may force you to change your attitude toward distribution, marketing, warehousing, etc.

The importance of a properly constructed business plan cannot be emphasized enough. Whether your proposed venture or existing operation is a small part-time operation or of substantial scale, develop a business plan to find where you stand. In this regard, I recommend that you purchase a publication entitled *How to Prepare a Business Plan*. It is available from the Institute for New Enterprise Development and it will cost you $15.00. This is the most complete guide describing the business plan that I have ever seen. It can be purchased by writing to:

Institute for New Enterprise Development
P.O. Box 360
Cambridge, Massachusetts 02138

Chapter VI

Motivation Is the Key

What Do You Want to Be When You Grow Up

Many of our aspirations have roots extending all the way back into childhood. We all know of little boys and girls who wanted to be presidents, astronauts, baseball players, premier dancers, and managers. Of course, these aspirations evolve and become more mature and reasonable as time passes, but they are still aspirations nonetheless. As one approaches mid-life and the realization of unfulfilled aspirations become apparent, a change in personality may be in the making. Unfortunately, some refer to this phase as the "mid-life crisis."

Whatever the case, there seems to be somewhat of a relationship between unfulfilled aspirations and entrepreneuring. Many individuals reach a critical point in their lives when they notice that most of their personal and professional goals have not been achieved. Some of these people, in order to avoid frustration, will seek to correct this situation. Many turn to entrepreneurship. Research has shown that most entrepreneurs take the plunge between the late twenties and late thirties, somewhere in the midst of mid-life.

Now, much has been written about people who "rock the boat" at mid-life. Even if you find yourself dominated by a tyrannical boss in a deadbeat job without hope of achieving much more than a mediocre salary, any attempt to make a try for change will be met with various forms of resistance. If you don't believe me, ask your boss for a raise or tell him/her that you want credit for your accomplishments. Sit back and watch the manure hit the fan. Or the next time you're having

Sunday dinner with the in-laws, make an announcement that you are going to quit your job and start your own business. Watch mother dear choke on her food while your spouse begins to harp about a regular paycheck. Your father-in-law will probably lecture you about family security.

What you must remember is that our society has cultural norms and systems that promote societal conformity. Churches and corporations are but a few examples. Any attempt to break with a norm will be met with some resistance. In addition, systems managers, who I sometimes refer to as "status-quo quacks," will do anything to preserve the system. You must realize that the system has taken care of these people, sometimes generously, and they are not about to let the system down.

There have been some books published of late suggesting that midlifers who are seeking changes and new experiences because of unrealized aspirations have not really grown up and are immature children at heart. Now, isn't that a childish notion? And even if it's true, so what? There is nothing wrong with reaching out to achieve one's life-long goals, and don't let anybody tell you differently. Those pop psychologists of the establishment are as dead as the liberal persuasions they embrace. They would do well to remember the old adage, "You don't stop playing because you grow old, you grow old because you stop playing."

Don't let anyone dissuade you. If you've got the entrepreneural itch, consider taking the plunge. And if you feel like a big kid for thinking about it—congratulations. You are taking your first steps toward economic independence. Put on your baseball cap, slide into your shorts, and hop on the old bike (ten-speed, I hope) and take a spin onto the wild winds of entrepreneurship.

The Many Faces of Motivation

The journey to entrepreneurial success has many roads, but they are all traveled by people who are motivated for one reason or another. Our research and those studies compiled by the Center for Entrepreneurial Management (CEM) show that 90 percent or more of the successful entrepreneurs queried stated they had either a desire to "work for themselves" or aspirations to "make money." The discussions below will review in detail the various motivations that stimulate entrepreneurs into action. Even though two stand out predominantly, most of the others are secondary motivations that may exist simultaneously.

DESIRE FOR CHANGE

Venture magazine reports that many people, upon reaching their thirties or forties will shade their corporate careers in favor of entrepreneurship. These people go through a rigorous process in order to view themselves in a new light. Many do away with ingrained philosophies and attempt to experiment with new ways of doing things.

I think that Jeffrey A. Timmons, a professor of entrepreneurial studies at Babson College, hit the nail on the head when he was quoted in *The New York Times* as saying, "The big corporation was Nirvana for a whole post-war generation. There was an implicit faith and trust in these huge corporations. But that love affair with bigness and big business insitutions blew apart during Vietnam."

Another big factor that has contributed to the desire for change is the economic environment. Beginning in the 1970s and continuing up to today, giant domestic corporations face a triple enemy. Foreign competition, high interest rates, and increasingly discriminating consumers loom large and are constant threats to real profits. Corporations have reacted by eliminating positions, cutting back other resources, and consolidating product lines.

The net effect of these actions can be observed by noting that out of the 20 million new jobs created in the U. S. over the last decade only 122,000 were generated by the country's one thousand largest companies. As the population growth of potential corporate executives (those in their thirties and forties) continues to exceed the growth in corporate employment opportunities, frustration will ensue. Less than patient baby boomers generally become upset at the notion of not obtaining what they consider appropriate standards of living. Nonexistent or slow-in-coming pay increases, bonuses, and promotions may not in themselves trigger mass entrepreneurial mania. But the stark realities of broken promises, vanishing job security, and the final realization that great wealth accumulation is reserved for those few who make it to the upper echelon of top management, are generally enough to start the entrepreneurial wheels in motion.

So, if you feel victimized by the so-called "system," spread your wings and soar into the realm of entrepreneurship. Many have come before you and there will be millions to follow. However, even though your desire for change may be an admirable motivation, that in itself will not guarantee entrepreneurial success. Entrepreneurship is as risky, if not more so, as life in the corporate nest. Investigation and knowledge are your biggest weapons that will ensure a better-than-even chance of success in your own business.

DESIRE FOR FAME

According to the Center for Entrepreneurial Management (CEM), 4 percent of the entrepreneurs they surveyed stated that their primary reason for embarking upon entrepreneurship was the desire for fame. Without a doubt, the limelight is a powerful motivating force, but we should not be blinded by it. Surely we would all like to be Ted Turner, T. Boone Pickens, or Frank Perdue. These self-made entrepreneurial successes are a rare breed who have created huge financial empires. Their endeavors have attracted media attention, thereby captivating the minds of millions. However, pursuing entrepreneurship for the pure sake of capturing fame is no less risky than going over Niagara Falls in a barrel in order to attract attention.

Generally, fame is a secondary consequence of achieving a high degree of entrepreneurial success. Seeking notoriety for the sake of notoriety is a precarious undertaking normally leading to less than careful planning. In extreme cases of glory seeking, shooting from the hip and impulsiveness will replace rational decision making. If General Custer could communicate from the other world, he would tell you as much. However, other entrepreneurial generals such as Patton, MacArthur, and Jackson were glory seekers, but their fame was predicated upon forward thinking and sound strategy.

Now, don't get the wrong idea here. The adage which states, "Boldness is the essence of strategy," is as true today as it was decades ago, but don't be fooled into thinking that sheer confidence will guarantee entrepreneurial success. The complexity of the business world today dictates that bold action be coupled with sound planning.

DESIRE FOR INDEPENDENCE

Herein lies one of the greatest secrets to entrepreneurial success. Studies conducted by the Center for Entrepreneurial Management (CEM) and research compiled for this book both conclude that a majority of successful entrepreneurs cited as their primary reason for pursuing entrepreneurship the desire to work for themselves. The CEM research showed 56 percent of those queried stated that they started a business because they didn't like working for someone else. Our studies confirmed the CEM findings in showing that approximately 60 percent said or implied the same thing. Without a doubt, a deep, heartfelt desire to be independent of an employer goes a long way in ensuring entrepreneurial success.

Below are listed some selected comments from successful entrepreneurs whom we queried for this book.

"I don't like working for the other man when I can make more money to secure my family's future."

"Well, I learned it was hard to get ahead or have anything beyond the necessities unless you work for yourself. . . . "

"I'm my own boss . . . there are no limitations placed on my ability to succeed. . . . "

"I hate to punch a time clock."

"I don't like bosses."

"By working for yourself you are not bound by corporate rules and limitations. There are no limits to what you can do for yourself when you work for yourself."

" . . . underhanded corporate practices."

"It's the pride of knowing it's yours."

"Well, I'm the boss. I never was much for taking orders."

" . . . more freedom in the working environment."

In essence, when working for somebody else, you are selling yourself for wholesale so that your employer can market the fruits of your labor at retail while at the same time keeping all of the profits. It's a hell of a note, but that's what keeps the system going. A study of entrepreneurs sponsored by Control Data Business Centers in conjunction with *Venture* magazine showed that most successful entrepreneurs initiated their first business, not because of a perceived market or a great idea, but because they felt ripped-off by previous employers. Even after making the transition to entrepreneurs, many still harbor ill feelings towards former employers and bosses.

In this country, more than 8 percent of the workforce has found the need to break away from the economic chains placed on them by their employers. They seek to be in business for themselves for the sake of independence and the right to absorb the full benefits of their labors.

You too must be motivated and inspired by visions of independence. If you are overly worried about collecting that regular paycheck or not happy with the prospects of throwing away the "security blanket" provided by your employer, I wholeheartedly recommend that you forget about entrepreneurship. You really have to be in love with the notion that you will be independent and free of employer restraints.

DESIRE FOR POWER

Henry Kissinger once implied that "power" was the ultimate "aphrodisiac." Without a doubt, power has an alluring and mystical quality that can drive people to do some strange and/or awesome things. In the business world, the word power is sometimes viewed in a negative light. Consequently, the words "control" and/or "influence" are used in its place.

As a successful entrepreneur you will find yourself possessing certain control prerogatives. For example, you can exercise influence or control over your employees. As your business and bank accounts grow, so will your influence with bankers and vendors. But don't allow the alluring characteristics of power to cloud your thinking or judgment. It is very tempting to allow ego to interdict sound reasoning. To illustrate, I used to work as an officer for a small savings and loan association. The CEO was an aging entrepreneur who suffered from insecurity problems stemming from childhood. He was short, and was raised by two aunts that spoiled him rotten. In addition, at one point during his professional life he was discharged from a position. He never dealt successfully with these personal flaws and failures. Therefore, the earlier mishaps manifested themselves in his decision-making. Exercising control over others was his escape from the past. He would issue orders and commands without good reason, and most did not achieve any meaningful purpose. When I would question him about his behavior he would fly off into a fit of rage. He would throw books and papers across the room and kick the walls of his office. Finally, this unstable personality threatened me with my career if I ever questioned his "authority" again.

Another case deals with the president of a small church-related college in New York. Upon coming on board as president, he immediately gutted the authority of the faculty. He ordered that the faculty committees would no longer be policy-generating bodies but would instead become policy-recommending mechanisms. In other words, he proclaimed himself college dictator. He argued that this action was necessary in the name of organizational efficiency. The organizational structure became cumbersome and it was obviously designed to stifle faculty initiatives and policy recommendations. Any ideas or recommendations suggesting or even hinting that some authority should be given back to the faculty was struck down in the name of "academic control." Faculty morale plunged at this institution largely because the president could not deal with his feelings of insecurity. His unwillingness to delegate authority is contributing to the slow demise of this fine institution of higher learning.

Understand power for what it really is—a privilege that has been acquired because of your entrepreneurial success. It must be used wisely and in a sensible manner. To exercise control for the sake of ego gratification or for reasons of insecurity is an abuse of power and it will lead you down the wrong path.

DESIRE FOR SECURITY

Ten years ago there was no link between employment security and entrepreneurship. In fact, quitting your job back then and starting your own business was considered something less than a secure thing to do. Oh, how times have changed!

Life is no longer sweet and secure in corporate America. Many millions of jobs, both in the blue- and white-collar sectors, are being displaced or slated for termination. Companies everywhere are economizing in order to meet the triple threats of international competitors, high interest rates, and discriminating consumers.

When I tell my students about job displacement within corporate America, they look at me somewhat perplexed. It is as if they don't really believe that Ford Motor Company, Eastman Kodak, and AT&T are going to terminate 20 percent of their workforces. Of course, the career placement directors within most colleges and universities are telling students to look for jobs with big companies. They cite high salaries, good benefits, and job security as reasons to seek out large companies. The average person on the street also seems to have difficulty accepting the notion that giant corporations, in general, are no longer safe havens of employment security.

Many disenfranchised corporate people are opting for entrepreneurship as a way of providing income and security for their families. However, don't be fooled by the number of individuals entering into the entrepreneurial ranks. Just because everybody is doing it doesn't mean that the risks are any less imposing. In fact, here we find ourselves right smack in the middle of the greatest economic and entrepreneurial boom in our country's history, and the government just reported that the number of small business failures has jumped 19 percent over last year. Many displaced corporate executives who have experienced entrepreneurship are calling it quits and are trying to get back into the corporate suites.

The point to keep in mind here is that as corporate jobs become more precarious relative to entrepreneurial endeavors, there will be a flight into the field of self-employment. But this doesn't change the need for sound thinking and planning before you take the plunge.

DESIRE FOR SEX

The renown psychologist, Sigmund Freud, conducted many empirical studies on human sexuality. His findings and conclusions would suggest that sex is a powerful motivating factor in all of us. We all know individuals who would do anything to impress or attract members of the opposite sex. To what degree there is a correlation between successful entrepreneurship and an active sex life is open to debate. We do know that many people experiment with entrepreneurship during the so-called "mid-life" crisis years, when some of these individuals seek out and experience new sexual adventures. There are even venture capitalists who subscribe to the notion that entrepreneurship and sexual activity go hand in hand. A. David Silver, a famous venture capitalist and author, suggested in an April 19, 1978, article published by the periodical *Chicago Business,* that successful entrepreneurs tended to be dominated by "achievement oriented mothers" and have "extraordinary sex drives." I know other venture capitalists who also believe this to be true. Now keep in mind that venture capitalists deal with a "particular" breed of entrepreneur—one who is geared to generating rapid growth and high profits.

Most entrepreneurs would acknowledge the powerful role that sex plays in our lives. However, I think they would discount the relationship between entrepreneurship and sex. This is not to suggest that a correlation doesn't exist. If it does, more than likely it would be found on an unconscious plane that would only surface upon direct query. In other words, don't ask.

Desire for Wealth

According to research conducted by the Center for Entrepreneurial Management (CEM), 34 percent of the entrepreneurs they queried (2500 in number) indicated that their primary motivation for starting a business is to make money. Without a doubt, wealth creation is a powerful motivating force when it comes to entrepreneurship, but as the aforementioned statistic would suggest, it is far from the most important.

The research conducted for this book would seem to uphold the CEM finding. However, this doesn't mean that you should feel guilty for wanting to be wealthy. Just keep in mind that, on the average, the successful entrepreneur earns about the same amount of money as a mid-level executive in a large corporation. And they both work long hours. So, don't let prospects of wealth be your only guiding light. Surely, quite a few people hit on a good idea or spot a forthcoming trend or fad and take advantage of it while making a potful of money. But these are the exceptions and not the norm.

Desire to Win

"Everyone loves a winner"—so goes the old cliché. Without a doubt, winning is contagious and a powerful motivator. However, the whole concept of "winning" must be put into proper perspective and analyzed.

Many entrepreneurs have reported that they have experienced one or more business failures before hitting the mark. Maybe of greater significance is the fact that research has shown that more than a few successful entrepreneurs were deprived as children. These early challenges gave them an incredible will to win. A. David Silver, the famous and well-respected venture capitalist mentioned earlier, notes in his book, *The Entrepreneurial Life: How to Go for It and Get It,* that many successful entrepreneurs experienced a lack of social interaction and some educational arrest in their early years. Also, Silver explains that many were sickly in nature, had less wealth than their peers, and were small in physical build. In my own experience, I have noted that many entrepreneurs do in fact seem to be short and have small physical characteristics. Thomas J. Stanley, the author of the *National Affluent Study,* lends support to Silver's remarks by implying that successful people tend to have deprived childhoods. Stanley states, " . . . adversity is a better trainer and disciplinarian than anything else." Silver also credits some entrepreneurial successes to "achievement-oriented mothers" who press their offsprings to succeed. Douglas MacArthur, who is now recognized as an entrepreneurial general, would have attested to this fact.

I believe that all entrepreneurs who really want to succeed possess a "winning spark." They can build upon past failures, misfortune, and personal flaws to reach great heights. Before becoming a mega-entrepreneur, media mogul Ted Turner took over his father's advertising business. The business was floundering and his dad committed suicide, yet Ted went on to build a thriving business. Our own President Reagan was raised in a poor household dominated by an alcoholic father. His success speaks for itself.

All you need to do is remember and learn from your hardships and to frankly address your shortcomings and then find the spark that will thrust you into the realm of entrepreneurship. Never forget where you come from or where you are going.

Guilt can also motivate people to win, especially guilt generated through marriage and divorce, according to Silver. We do know that many people embark upon entrepreneurship during the years described as "mid-life." Unfortunately, it is a time of life in which marriages tend to come under heavy pressures and consequently many divorces ensue. Psychologists warn us that difficult marriages and divorces can leave psychological scars. Many people feel guilty about the breakup of their family and will label themselves "failures" because of their inability to make a marriage work. Sometimes this guilt will manifest itself in the form of entrepreneurial spirit. A disenchanted or disenfranchised spouse may seek to prove to himself/herself and to others, in particular the other spouse and children, that he/she is not a loser and that they can make it on their own and still be a good provider. However, and in another family realm, success may divide families in the worst of ways, rekindling sibling competition and creating guilt because of outperforming Mom and Dad.

Motivate Yourself to Success

There is no set formula that guarantees to stimulate your entrepreneurial motivation. In the previous section, we discussed some widely held beliefs about why people seek out entrepreneurship. Obviously, a healthy and constructive dislike for your employer definitely provides a push. Likewise, other factors influence the decision to take the plunge. Whatever the case, you have to decide what motivates you the most and then play on those stimulations. Visualize where you want to be in five or ten years and keep those objectives before you consistently. And just remember, "The only thing to it is to do it."

Chapter VII

History Is Important

The Legacy of Mom and Dad

Some research studies have linked successful entrepreneurship to common background traits. Data compiled by the Center for Entrepreneurial Management (CEM) has shown that some interesting patterns may exist. Sixteen percent of the entrepreneurs interviewed by CEM indicated that at least one parent experienced entrepreneurship at some point in his or her life. A large 36 percent indicated that at least 1 parent was self-employed for most of the working years. Another 10 percent said both parents had experienced entrepreneurship in some part of their lives while 4 percent indicated that both parents were self-employed most of their working years. Thirty-five percent acknowledged that neither parent experienced entrepreneurship. In total, 66 percent of those entrepreneurs queried showed some degree of parental involvement in entrepreneurial endeavors.

Having parents that are or were entrepreneurs can go a long way in making the road to entrepreneurship easier. In addition, the psychological support never hurts.

Roots

The CEM study mentioned above found that 36 percent of those entrepreneurs responding indicated that at least one grandparent was born abroad. Ten percent acknowledged that one or both parents were born outside the U. S. and 7 percent said that they (the entrepreneurs queried) were born in another country. Forty-seven percent felt that foreign roots were not important when considering entrepreneurial success.

Escaping economic and political repression, many immigrants came to America to take part in her economic miracle. Upon arriving in the so-called "promised land," many found another type of economic slavery so well depicted in Upton Sinclair's book, *The Jungle*. Many industrial companies took advantage of their naive interpretation of wage freedom. Some historians feel that this is the reason for the beginning of the Italian Mafia in America. The young Italian immigrant boys were looking for a better life only to find discrimination and economic deprivation. So they decided to make a life of their own in what they considered a system dominated by a very few corrupt Anglo-Saxon industrialists and bankers. In other words, they wanted some of the action for themselves.

Don't get the wrong idea here. Quite a few immigrants reacted to the conditions they found in America in a positive way—starting their known enterprises. Many have passed this entrepreneuring spirit on to their descendants. Even today, many immigrants who are just arriving here are making entrepreneurial history. The Koreans in Philadelphia and the Vietnamese in San Francisco are currently making a big splash.

One thing is perfectly clear in this analysis. Immigrants of the present or recent past (last 85 years) and their recent descendants (two succeeding generations) seem to be more prone to entrepreneuring than people not possessing this background. Of course, this is not indicative of entrepreneurial success by any means. It just suggests that individuals with immigrant roots going back further than two generations on both sides of the family tend to become more ingrained in the American business culture. They are more prone to take for granted the economic fruits of America and less willing to risk entrepreneurship.

Mother Dearest

In the previous chapter I mentioned that some venture capitalists feel that achievement-oriented mothers are strong motivating forces. Many a mother has pushed her offspring to accomplish great entrepreneurial feats. We all know that, right? However, many psychologists are presently giving some credit to the "old man." Baseball great Pete Rose attributes his success to his father. John Fleming, a ship owner and one of the entrepreneurs interviewed for this book, states, "My father is largely responsible for my success..."

Recent research has shown that an increasing number of successful entrepreneurs are reporting that they had a comfortable relationship with the parent who provided most of the family's income (generally the father). In fact, according to research conducted by the CEM, 53 percent reported a comfortable relationship while 29 percent indicated it was strained. Nine percent acknowledged a competitive relationship.

Some heated debates have been sparked over this issue. Now, it is not the objective of this book to take sides in the "battle of the sexes," but most experts would agree that mothers have more influence in shaping personality than do fathers. I have a friend who illustrates this situation perfectly. His mother is a typical white Anglo-Saxon Protestant who believes that "security" in employment should reign supreme and that risking time and/or money is unwise. On the other hand, the father, who was an entrepreneur for most of his life, advised his son differently. These differences made for some interesting home entertainment. Guess what? Mama won out. This friend of mine who desperately wants to own his own business is so overcome with the "security syndrome" that he cannot commit himself to take the plunge. He has the ability, but Mama so warped his entrepreneurial instincts that not even Dad's encouragement could help out at this point.

The ideal situation of course is to come from a household where both parents or the only parent possesses some forward thinking or insight. Parents who encourage "reasonable" experimentation do more for their children than the sum total of other positive environmental stimuli. And if you come from a household that is definitely "anti-entrepreneurial," just keep in mind that most of our parents were children of the Depression era or were nurtured in an environment dominated by large corporations and job security. Take their negative comments with caution and do what you think is best.

Other Considerations*

Research has shown that 51 percent of successful entrepreneurs have been fired from one or more jobs. This is really not surprising

*The statistics mentioned in this section were made available by the Center for Entrepreneurial Management.

considering the fact that entrepreneurs are rebels at heart and boat rockers who don't like working for other people. In addition, it is known that many entrepreneurs, about 62 percent of them, had career experience with employers who had less than 100 employees. Fifteen percent had prior career experience with employees having between 100 and 500 workers. Obviously, these entrepreneurs had an appreciation for the trials and tribulations of small business management from the very start.

Also, it is known that successful entrepreneurs tend to be the oldest child in the family in approximately 60 percent of the cases. Likewise, many entrepreneurs experimented with business ventures as children. Almost 75 percent of those researched indicated having operated a childhood venture. It would seem that the seed of entrepreneurship can be planted in children, and if allowed to germinate this seed can sprout entrepreneurial rewards later in life.

Take the Plunge Anyway

Don't worry if your parent(s) lacked entrepreneurial exposure. Likewise, not having any immigrants in your recent ancestral lineage should not be disheartening to you. And don't be upset if you were not the oldest child in your family or you never worked for a small firm. Surely, having been exposed to entrepreneuring parents and/or grandparents from the "old country" who fled economic and political repression to pick the fruits of American opportunity may help mold you into an entrepreneur. Without a doubt, being exposed to any entrepreneurial environment is a plus in your favor. However, if you are lacking those experiences, just remember what was discussed in earlier chapters. Entrepreneurship is more a learned experience than anything else. It can be taught and absorbed. Now, there are born entrepreneurs without question, but most are just ordinary people. This accounts for the large number of individuals, with many different backgrounds and traits, who can be labeled successful entrepreneurs.

Chapter VIII

Persistence and Initiative Pay Dividends

Seize the Market

Given the highly charged and competitive marketplace, you can expect to compete with experienced, well-trained, and organized competitors. To a large degree, survival will be contingent upon your ability to locate marketing potentials and then to move on them quickly and efficiently. Consequently, you must be ever alert to changes or modification in your market(s) so as to beat your competitors to the punch.

Taking the Bull by the Horns

It's not enough to identify changes in your market and select local opportunities. You must be prepared to quickly pounce on the prey in a profitable manner. Here is where we separate the men from the boys. Through the years I have seen dozens of entrepreneurs fail to act upon apparently profitable opportunities for many reasons that cannot be adequately explained within the confines of this book. However, one reason stands out predominantly, and that is the "fear of failure."

Now, I do not advise that you jump at every opportunity for the sake of dealing with your fears. But the constant unwillingness to make a decision even after completing a proper investigation of· an opportunity (methods are discussed later in this book) is paramount to laying the foundation of entrepreneurial demise. At some point you have to take the bull by the horns.

Sweat Buys Equity

You are about to read the most important section of this book. It deals with the subject of "persistence" as it relates to entrepreneurship. When conducting the research for this book, I asked a question relating to factors that lead to entrepreneurial success. Seventy percent of those queried stated or implied that persistence and perseverance were the most important elements. Below are some quotes from a few of the entrepreneurs researched:

"I attribute my success to a lot of hard work and determination."
"Dedication to hard work."
"Persistence."
"Drive."
"Stick-to-itiveness and never giving up."
"Perseverance."
"Perseverance and hard work."
"Long hours and hard work."
"Hard work."
"Patience and perseverance."
"Be thoroughly dedicated."

Experts in the field of entrepreneurship are sure about one thing—the more you persist the greater the chance of succeeding at entrepreneurial endeavors. In addition, we know from research provided by Dun & Bradstreet and illustrated in Table 3, that the longer you are in business for yourself the less chance you have of failure. And there is another thing to consider here. If you sell your business at some point in the future, you will find that there is generally a direct relationship between price and longevity. A longer life will attract a higher price.

"Staying the course" can pay dividends, as President Reagan has often said. And he should know, being one who has fought for his program and beliefs without giving in to much compromise. Reagan, like other entrepreneurs who persist, are reaping the rewards of steadfast planning, confidence, and unparalleled faith in their decisions.

Strategic Dollars

I have already discussed the importance of strategic planning to the entrepreneur in an earlier chapter. However, it is my responsibility to

TABLE 3

AGE OF BUSINESS FAILURE—1983

Age In Years	Percentage of Total Failures
Five Years Or Less	47.0
Six To Ten Years	30.2
Over Ten Years	22.8

Source: "The Business Failure Record." By permission of Dun & Bradstreet Credit
   Services, a company of The Dun & Bradstreet Corporation.

convey the link between persistence and strategic planning. An increasing number of smaller firms are involved in strategic planning for obvious reasons. If conducted properly, it will help you to focus on your present and future markets and give you the incentive to be more patient while laying the foundations to ensure long-term profits and survival. *The Wall Street Journal* recently acknowledged this by stating "...the notion of strategic planning, long practiced by big U. S. companies, is percolating down to smaller concerns. Owners are taking a longer-term view of their companies and a more disciplined approach to analyzing the players in their markets."

Short-Term Suicide

Don't fall prey to your impulsive desires and aspirations. There are already too many people in this country chasing get-rich-quick schemes and the like. The slipshod and second-rate reign supreme today largely due to quick market decisions and a less than adequate commitment to quality and the long term. These individuals, given the increasingly charged competitive environment, will not survive to see tomorrow.

Whether you are already in business or a prospective entrepreneur, just keep in mind that jumping from one idea, product, or service to another will generally lead to failure and frustration. You need to concentrate and focus your energies on specific and stable objectives. Of course, there are individuals who can spot trends and take advantage of them quickly. They have the ability to get in and out with amazing speed. Now, most of us do not possess this quality. In this regard, it would be wise to investigate opportunities thoroughly and then persist when it makes good sense. However, always keep alert as to changes in the marketplace and be prepared to alter your plans as the environment dictates. Oftentimes, guarded flexibility, with long-term objectives always in mind, is a better alternative than "turning on a dime." Moving too quickly presents the danger of overreaction and miscalculation.

Never Say Never

Pete Rose, the famed and self-effacing baseball player, will tell you that he is just an average person. He attributes his success to persistence and perseverance.

Several weeks ago, I came across an Associated Press article concerning the television series, "Star Trek." The article went on to quote the creator, Gene Roddenberry, as saying, "When Star Trek was first shown on television it was so unpopular that my own father watched it, went out, walked up and down the street and apologized to all the neighbors." Of course, the network stuck it out and the rest is history. More recently, the television show "Hill Street Blues" was not a popular show in its infancy. NBC almost cancelled it, but decided to "stay the course," and today the network is highly acclaimed for presenting such a fine show to the American public.

Also, in the world of entertainment, we have the late country music queen, Patsy Cline. She came from humble beginnings and lived on the wrong side of the tracks in Winchester, Virginia. In the late 1940s and 1950s she resided on Kent Street, an area of Winchester that had a large concentration of blacks and poor whites. She had a beautiful voice and would sing in any tavern that would give her a booking. She was outspoken and at times ran with some questionable people. This led the people of Winchester, a small, conservative, and quiet town, to reject and even disown her in some ways. Even today, many people in Winchester scorn her and there are those who refuse to go along with the renaming of a street in her honor. This jealousy is unbecoming a community that at one point in its history elected George Washington to his first public office. Patsy never gave up and always thought in big terms. It was this drive that took her to Nashville, where she found success and fame. Patsy was also responsible for the discovery of another great country music talent known to all as Loretta Lynn.

Many of our presidents in their earlier careers suffered humiliating defeats and crushing blows only to bounce back stronger than ever.

This better prepared them to meet and overcome the challenges that lay before them. In fact, the difficult early years built a strong foundation that supported their efforts in achieving the highest office in the land.

I will end this chapter by stating that, without a doubt, you too can become a successful entrepreneur. First, you need an objective. Write it down. Second, you must visualize the objective and see yourself accomplishing it. Third, keep on pushing, trying, investigating, and experimenting until you hit upon the right combination that will unlock the realm of entrepreneurship. It may take years and several tries, but in the final analysis you will find that your greatest ally was "persistence."

Chapter IX

Harnessing People Profits

Employees Are Income Generators

Employees are your most important resource. As an entrepreneur you will soon realize that salary and wages will be your single largest expense factor. The way in which you manage your human resources will determine the degree to which you are successful as an entrepreneur. In other words, human productivity will make or break you. It's not an easy resource to manage. Research has shown that about 75 percent of all workers are unhappy with their jobs. In addition, entrepreneurial firms have fewer resources per employee than do larger companies. Consequently, this complicates the employee morale problems for small enterprises.

Once you realize that employees are income generators after reaching a certain level of output, you will note that it is impossible to survive without them. Another factor you must consider is the growing employee shortages that are starting to appear throughout the country in all occupational classifications. This is due to the accelerating economy. Enhanced employment-related competition among all employers will make it difficult and costly to keep good employees. That doesn't make life simpler for the new or existing entrepreneur.

Building a Positive Environment

"Happy employees are productive employees." The old adage is true. If you treat your employees fairly and give them the respect they deserve, only positive results can ensue. As a management consultant,

I have found that in many troubled companies the difference between profit and loss is not so much material in nature as it is human. Most successful entrepreneurs know this to be a fact.

You will find that employee management can be a challenging affair. Below are listed some helpful ideas that may assist you in fostering a productive and profitable employee relations program.

COMMUNICATIONS

Do you know that most divorces occur because of the lack of communication between spouses? Likewise, many employer/employee partings are due to communication voids within organizations. You must give your employees the opportunity to express their feelings, ideas, and viewpoints. This must be done in an environment absent of fear and retaliation. But this is a two-lane highway. Not only must you develop a work environment that allows freedom of expression, you must not be fearful of what your employees have to say. Employees are generally a valuable source of information. For some reason that cannot be easily explained, you will find that your employees will see things that you do not. Opportunities and cost-saving methods are at times very apparent to employees, but not to the entrepreneur.

This brings to mind a company in which the young CEO refused to heed the advice of his employees concerning the financial manager. He was ineffective and somewhat less than competent and had friends on the board of directors. Not only did this CEO fail to act upon his employees' advice, but he promoted the financial officer and even involved himself in some questionable financial-related decision-making because he lacked experience in this area. Eventually, the CEO had to fire this financial manager because of gross financial mis-management. Guess what? That old thick-skinned financial manager got himself some hard-hitting lawyers and told the CEO, "If I go, you go." He had a good argument. The current CEO, as well as former CEOs, had ordered him to do a lot of the things that led to his termination. The CEO, instead of taking the heat and a few bruises, hired this guy back in another capacity at approximately one-half of his previous salary. But here's the kicker. This guy never comes to work, except to pick up his paycheck, and he will continue to do this until retirement. Not only that, he's working as a vice-president for another organization.

This CEO is living a lie and is unwilling to risk the consequences of revealing the truth. He should have listened to his employees in the very beginning. Unfortunately, this experience has practically destroyed the morale of his employees.

As a management consultant, I normally recommend that entrepreneurs should meet with their employees once a week. Meeting more often than that is a waste of time that generally leads to meaningless discussion. Of course, the exception to this would be if there is an organizational crisis that demands immediate attention. If the organization has grown so large that it is impossible to meet with your employees on a regular basis, it would be wise to delegate that responsibility to your other managers and supervisors. They could then report to you on a periodic schedule.

However, just keep in mind that nothing replaces the personal touch. Your employees crave it. Look at the chairman and president of Toyota Motors. They spend four hours a day on the assembly line with their workers. No, they don't help make the cars. Their purpose is simple. They *listen* to the employees. This is in stark contrast to a small college in northwestern Pennsylvania where the president and the chief academic officer are seldom seen near faculty offices or classrooms. They meet with the faculty once a month, generally to dispense negative information. Now, there is no excuse for this behavior. This college employs no more people than the personnel department of a large corporation.

There is another point that you should consider. Never, and I emphasize never, lie to your employees. It's like lying to the media— they never forget. Some managers feel that there are economic benefits to be gained from not telling the truth to their employees. Some justify their actions by rationalizing that if lying is for the good of the system or organization, it is okay to do. This process can become contagious, and if you consistently utilize this tactic it will come home to haunt you. Employee loyalty and morale will be affected in a negative way. Lying will cost you more in terms of lost productivity and employee turnover than any gains that could ever be realized. And you never know, it could even attract media attention!

DELEGATION OF AUTHORITY

It is only human nature to want control over one's own destiny. As an entrepreneur you know this to be a fact concerning yourself. However, it is also true of your employees. They want input into decisions that affect their employment situation. They may not express this desire overtly, but if you ask them, watch the flood gates open.

Entrepreneurs by their very nature usually take a "theory X" approach to decision-making. Many want to be firmly in control. Quite a few believe that employees work only for reasons of economic salvation and are not willing or capable enough to make decisions. If you back them into a corner concerning employee participation they will praise the concept of "seat-of-the-pants" management and then criticize "participative" methods as being theoretical poppycock.

The other extreme, rare birds indeed, are the "theory Y" entrepreneurs. These believe that employees want and even crave decision-making responsibilities. They argue that if employees are challenged, results will ensue.

Now, I bet you think that my hat is going to end up in the corner of the "theory Y" entrepreneurs. Wrong. Both extremes are actually bad. We know that the complexity of the present and future business environment will not allow, for very long periods anyway, theory X approaches to business applications. Entrepreneurs seeking to foster total control for extended periods of time should heed the words of Dean William Inge, a British clergyman, who stated, "A man may build himself a throne of bayonets, but he cannot sit on it." Well, not for a long period of time anyway.

Entrepreneurs who use "theory Y" to an extreme risk losing control of the ship. Sears, Roebuck & Company experienced this very thing. The company decentralized and delegated decision-making authority as far down the employee ranks as they could get. Sears jumped on the "decentralization" bandwagon of the late 1960s and early 1970s. However, they went too far and lost control. Market shares and profits began to decline. As a management consultant, I have seen this happen to entrepreneurial firms as well. The entrepreneurs take a "laissez-faire" approach to decision-making, also known as "management-by-exception," and will only get involved in matters when a crisis or an exceptional situation unfolds. Here you have the makings of total loss of control.

What did Sears do to save itself? The company recentralized back to the divisional headquarters. After some restructuring Sears found a winning combination by utilizing both theory X and theory Y approaches. And this is what I recommend for entrepreneurial firms. You as an entrepreneur should do what is necessary to succeed and grow. That usually means marketing the hell out of your products or services. There will be little time for other things. Set your broad organizational goals and policies. Make sure you review them on a periodic basis so as to ensure their relevance. They will need to be modified on a regular basis. In addition, keep attuned to the external problems that may threaten your enterprise and be ready to move on problems before or after they appear.

Back in 1980 I worked on a consulting project where the entrepreneurs let their employees set all operating policies without providing any directions. When I took over, wages were spiraling out of control (increasing 20 percent annually), overtime abuse was rampant, workflow was decentralized, and, believe it or not, employee morale was shot. All of this was contributing to deteriorating profits. As consultant-in-charge, I recommended that wages be frozen and overtime approved only by special permission. Work assignments were centralized and unprofitable and/or ineffective employees were encouraged to leave. In fact, those employees that were taking advantage of the previous organizational chaos did, in fact, go elsewhere after the new system went into operation. Also, employees were required to set yearly objectives that would enhance the company's performance as well as their professional expertise. Salary, benefits, bonuses, and promotions were based on the successful attainment of those objectives. Finally, a professional business manager was recruited to administer the new system. Morale and productivity recovered to normal levels and so did profitability.

After you do the above-mentioned things, then let your employees take it from there. Allow them to set their own employment related objectives. Of course, make sure that their objectives are tuned to yours. Let them make some important decisions and don't be afraid to give them some control or authority. You will be surprised at the positive reactions in terms of employee morale and productivity. As you know, this translates into profits. Without a doubt, you will notice that more organizational problems can be successfully resolved by including your employees in the decision-making process.

A young lady entrepreneur, who owns two fast-food establishments and was interviewed for this book, hit the nail on the head when she said, "You must have the ability to pull the best out of others, to find good employees and give them a certain amount of autonomy." This gal is planning for rapid expansion and is including, as one of her goals, a plan for her employees to have ownership interest in the business.

HYGIENE

Organizational hygiene, as traditionally used to stimulate employee
motivation, refers to such things as employee-management relations,
managerial policies, salaries and benefits, working conditions, etc.
The term "hygiene," as it relates to human motivation and its
application to the working environment, was coined by the famed
management expert Frederick Herzberg. He argued that if organizational hygiene is not up to par it will have a negative impact on
employee morale and productivity. What's worse, from your standpoint, is the fact that Herzberg implies that clearing up organizational
hygiene does not create a gain in terms of human motivation. In other
words, your employees will expect, at the very least, a decent place to
work.

My experiences in the consulting profession would lead me to
disagree with Herzberg somewhat. In projects where organizational
hygiene was substantially upgraded in terms of employee benefits,
incentives, and working conditions, I have noticed a definite enhancement of employee morale. For example, I managed a consulting
project where the employees didn't even have a decent place to eat their
lunch. Also, several national holidays were not honored in terms of
days off or pay. The first thing we did was give the employees a nice
lunch room and holidays off with pay. They responded in a positive
way almost immediately. Of course, in this case morale was so low that
the only place it could go was up. You could argue that reaching a
normal level of morale is really no gain at all. But you must consider
the implications of extremely low morale on productivity. If you can
reach an average stage of employee morale and motivation, the effort
will be worth it in terms of heightened productivity and profitability.

There is definitely one thing that you can count on here. If you do
not provide a work environment that is hygienically acceptable to your
employees, they will lose their self-respect. This will translate into
employment-related disinterest and contempt. Now, it's not their fault.
This is a normal defensive reaction that helps them maintain self-
esteem. If you refuse to recognize or deal with it in terms of
organizational hygiene, the costs will be great in the form of compromised quality, low productivity, and waste.

Just remember that employee apathy is usually not just a matter of
people unwilling to work hard. In most cases, it is just a normal

reaction by typical people operating in a less than acceptable hygienic environment. Generally, the cost of enhancing your firm's hygiene is more than offset by the effects you can expect in terms of improved employee morale and productivity. If you cannot afford to make the upfront investment necessary to improve organizational hygiene, be honest with your employees. They will understand if you are forthright. However, they will expect the investment to be made when you can afford it.

INCENTIVES

Incentives are the foundation of America's economic system and standard of living. The tax incentives provided in 1978 and 1981 are largely responsible for our current state of prosperity. They fostered a powerful drive to succeed and profit. China is currently experimenting with entrepreneurial and managerial incentives. The objective is to bring their economy out of the dark ages, and they are accomplishing this task with impressive flair.

In my opinion, incentives are the best tools to stimulate human productivity known to mankind. It is really amazing to note the number of large and small firms who have failed to realize this simple fact. This brings to mind a consulting project in which I participated as consultant-in-charge. This project was classified as a "turnaround" due to the nature of the difficulties that we faced. What really surprised me was the fact that this enterprise was managed by a very intelligent entrepreneur who never gave thought to the notion of employee incentives. When I mentioned the possibility of implanting incentive systems, the idea was immediately dismissed as "too expensive."

This guy was losing $13,000 a month. He was overemployed and his accounting system was in complete disarray. We got a handle on the financial books so that profits and losses could be detected by department. Previously the company simply put all of its revenues and expenses into one soup bowl. The entrepreneur did not know what department was making or losing money. After inputting a credible accounting system we systematically reduced employment where needed. Unfortunately, it involved a lot of displacement. Employee morale began to decline, but that is to be expected in the initial stages of a turnaround. About a week after the layoffs the entrepreneur and I had a meeting with the remaining employees. We told them that the former employees were drags on profits and productivity, thereby costing them in terms of wages, benefits, and working conditions. This was all true. In addition, they were informed of the need to work harder. For their cooperation and enhanced productivity, we promised that they would share in cost savings and profits. An incentive bonus system was established, and the rest is history. Productivity and earnings soared. The company began to generate $10,000–$20,000 a month in profits. Some of the employees earned an amount equal to 25 percent of their annual salaries in the form of performance bonuses.

Now, don't run out and think you are going to set the world on fire with an incentive system. An incentive program must be well thought out, like any other management decision, especially in terms of your own profitability. You do not want to pay bonuses and lose money at the same time. In the previous example, we identified a target return on investment for the company and it was 15 percent. Every department was encouraged to achieve that figure. Twenty-five percent of the departmental income generated over and above the income needed to make the 15 percent return that was given back to the employees. In other words, the incentive system imposed here not only paid for itself but also returned many times its cost in terms of productivity increases.

It is really impossible within the scope of this chapter to discuss all of the incentive programs that are available. Go out and find yourself some good books on management and operational techniques. Just keep in mind that an incentive system should be tailor-made to fit your entrepreneurial enterprise. Whatever the case, it is always wise to reward your employees for outstanding performance. To do less is damaging in terms of employee morale and your own profitability. I knew one entrepreneur who paid his employees a bonus for coming up with meaningful and verifiable cost savings ideas. He would pay them 15 percent of the annual savings for the first year, 10 percent the second year, and 5 percent in the third year.

Another incentive that is largely overlooked by entrepreneurs is called "praise." Some would argue that praise is not an incentive, but it does have the power to motivate. The famed Harvard psychologist B. F. Skinner proved through experimentation that positive reinforcement is a mighty motivator. So give your employees some credit and a consistent pat on the back. While you're at it, give yourself a pat also.

Employee Alliances

As an entrepreneur you are, in fact, a Jack-of-all-trades. You must manage, market, plan, produce, organize, etc. Time is at a premium and yours will be spread thin.

Draw upon the experience and knowledge base of your employees. If you ask and/or investigate, a reservoir of new ideas will surely appear. Many employees are just dying for the chance to make their suggestions known. Now, I am not referring to a "suggestion box" approach here. You need substantial personal contact with your employees. In other words, make the employees your partners. Absorb their ideas and use those that are appropriate. Give them some authority and decision-making rights. Let them help you manage and take the heat.

Entrepreneurial success is a two-way street where employees are involved. Your fortunes and those of the employees are interdependent. One cannot exist without the other for a very long period of time without compromising organizational productivity and effective operation.

Orientation Programs

As a bank officer, early in my career, I was shocked to discover the turnover rate of bank window tellers. Much of this turnover took place in the first two months of employment. Upon investigation, I was startled to find that many tellers quit because of reasons not related to traditional factors such as salary and benefits, which are normally low in the banking industry. Most were intimidated by the job. They were thrown into the "pit," so to speak, and left to the lions. Unable to adjust, many simply just quit.

Turnover is expensive in terms of lost investment. In the banking industry, it takes approximately six months to break even on a new teller. If they leave before that period of time, it's like throwing money out the window. After doing some research, I found that by developing and providing an orientation program, turnover could be reduced substantially. Unfortunately, this is the step where most entrepreneurs fail. Because of time constraints and other factors, many entrepreneurs just do not give enough thought to the importance of employee turnover in terms of cost savings. Believe me, it would pay you to spend some time with your new employees. Help them get used to their new environment and fellow workers. Provide some training over and above the proverbial "feeding them to the wolves." Large companies have learned that it pays to do this, and you should take the hint.

Forget About Those Japs

The American business community seems to be involved in a heated love affair with Japanese management practices. We praise their approaches to problem-solving and decision-making while criticizing our own methods. But there is an interesting point to ponder in all of this. Those so-called Japanese miracle cures were actually developed here in the United States. Back in the 1950s and 1960s, the Japanese government and business community sent thousands of their managers, officials, and students to the U. S. in order to learn American management practices. They returned to Japan with the best of our ideas and methods.

So why are they so much more effective at using new management concepts? The answer deals with application. The Japanese managers borrowed our creative approaches to product resolution and actually applied them to their managerial structures while the managers in the U. S. did nothing other than manage in the same old ways. Remember, the Japanese are great imitators. They let the United States and other countries spend the large amount of money needed to generate new approaches, ideas, and technologies. Because they are our allies, access to these new methods is readily available. Then they use what we have given them to compete against us in the international and domestic marketplace. There is really nothing wrong with this notion. However, the fact remains that we are not applying our own creative energies in the most innovative way.

If you observe closely, you will notice that Japanese firms have implanted only those American managerial principles that can be successfully applied in a homogeneous cultural environment. This is because they are a one-culture country, which makes life easier for the Japanese manager. He/she deals with just one set of attitudes, beliefs, and customs. This environment provides for a large degree of societal and employment-related conformity. Consequently, employee "individualism" is not encouraged. The system, be it the country, company, plant, or work group, is always viewed as being more important than the single employee. Individual goals are always subordinated to the objectives of the larger organization. In essence, Japan's economy can only be described as "state-controlled capitalism." A better name would probably be "corporate socialism."

Things are different here in America, even though we recognize the importance of the "system." Individualism is still a mighty force and it must be reckoned with in a reasonable way. Even the attempts of the corporate bureaucrats to force organizational conformity on their employees will never succeed. Their efforts will only cause morale problems and loss of productivity. Just remember that out of every employee group there will emerge one or two highly productive people who seem to carry the group, so to speak. To reward the group at the expense of the productive individual(s) is an economic crime.

Here in this country, individuals who stand above the crowd in a productive way expect to be rewarded. This incentive, based upon individual reward and initiative, is the hallmark of our great economic system and standard of living. Is it any wonder that Japan, facing mounting economic pressures and problems, is once again starting to show an interest in our creative and job-generating entrepreneurial economy.

American culture is heterogeneous in its make-up. We are a multiculture society—a "melting pot" of many different attitudes, backgrounds, beliefs, and goals. Conformity, Japanese style, is really impossible, given those conditions.

American firms, both large and small, need to develop their own unique approaches when dealing with their employees. Trying to copy Japanese managerial styles or even the methods of other domestic companies could be a hazardous undertaking.

Here Are Some Tips

Below are some tips for improving human relations within the entrepreneurial firm:*

1. Improve your own general understanding of human behavior.
2. Accept the fact that others do not always see things as you do.
3. In any differences of opinion, consider the possibility that you may not have the right answer.
4. Show your employees that you are interested in them and that you want their ideas on how conditions can be improved.

*U. S. Small Business Administration, Publication No. 3 entitled, *Human Relations in Small Business,* by Martin M. Bruce, Ph.D.

5. Treat your employees as individuals; never deal with them impersonally.
6. Respect differences of opinion.
7. Insofar as possible, give explanations for management actions.
8. Provide information and guidance on matters affecting employees' security.
9. Make reasonable efforts to keep jobs interesting.
10. Encourage promotion from within.
11. Express appreciation publicly for jobs well done.
12. Offer criticism privately, in the form of constructive suggestions for improvement.
13. Train supervisors to be concerned about the people they supervise, the same as they would be about merchandise or materials or equipment.
14. Keep your staff up-to-date on matters that affect them.
15. Quell false rumors, and provide correct information.
16. Be fair!

Look at the Difference

The comparison below* is interesting in terms of the difference between how employees think versus managers. Noting these variations will help you understand your employees' motivations more fully.

Ranking by Employees	What Employees Want	Ranking by Management
1	Credit for all work done	7
2	Interesting work	3
3	Fair pay	1
4	Understanding and appreciation	5
5	Counsel on personal problems	8
6	Promotion on merit	4
7	Good physical working conditions	6
8	Job security	2

Chapter X

Know What You're Selling

Knowledge Is the Key

"A good salesman can sell anything," so the story goes. Without a doubt, the consumer landscape is littered with thousands of useless gadgets and widgets that somehow seem to survive the severity of the buying public. Have you ever wondered how something like the "pet rock" could be successfully marketed? Well, I learned the hard way. Ten years ago while representing a client to a New York advertising firm, I was asked to describe why my client's product would be successful in the marketplace. While describing the product's attributes, I was suddenly stopped by the advertising executive in charge of our account. He snapped, "Damn it, it's not the product that sells, it's the concept built around the product." He went on to say, "People want to know how your product will make their life easier and/or more pleasant. The product itself is a secondary factor."

This is not to suggest that product or service knowledge should play a subordinate role to cosmetic considerations. On the contrary, knowledge of the product or service is necessary in order to project its conceptual utility. This is especially true where intangibles (services) are involved. In addition, as the product or service becomes more complicated, there is a need for enhanced knowledge of what you are selling. In many cases, the customer will want to be educated before purchasing.

There is nothing more frustrating than dealing with a salesperson who cannot answer questions about what he/she is trying to sell. Don't you fall victim to this trap. Know your product or service inside and out. When questioned, don't embarrass yourself by not knowing the answer. If you find yourself in a bind, make sure you have the capability of getting the right answer quickly.

Never Let Your Guard Down

It is very important to keep abreast of all changes that may have an effect on your product or service. Advances in technology may dictate a modification in your existing product/service lines. A product might have to be eliminated and a replacement found. In some cases, you may want to get out of a particular business altogether. For example, we have found that the bottom of the "satellite dish" market has fallen out. Many dish manufacturers, distributors, and retailers are hurting badly. They could have avoided hard times if many of them had paid attention to the handwriting on the wall. Well over two years ago a lot of noise was being generated by the satellite networks concerning the "stealing" of their programming by dish owners. The TV cable industry successfully petitioned the Federal Communications Commission in hopes of getting permission to "scramble" their signals. In other words, dish owners could not receive satellite network programming without first going through and paying their local cable system.

The above example is but one of many situations where dynamic environmental factors have changed the need and/or demand for a product in very short order. Its lesson is simple. You must consistently evaluate the external forces that impose themselves on your products/services. Modify, diversify, eliminate, or add when conditions warrant. To do less would be disastrous, to say the least.

Table 2 on page 75 has a list of external forces that an entrepreneurial firm might encounter.

Chapter XI

When in Doubt Look About

Controlling for Profits

You will always find successful managers looking over their shoulders. They utilize various methods that provide them with feedback data. This control information is used to help them manage more effectively. Now, this is where some entrepreneurs have difficulty. Many research studies have shown that some individuals who start their own businesses are not good managers. If these individuals do not rely on outside expertise or qualified employees, they're asking for trouble. Many go out of business or are forced to sell. Just remember that a good manager will spot and solve a problem before it can threaten the enterprise. Procrastination is deadly.

The following pages will help you identify some additional steps that are necessary to ensure entrepreneurial success.

The Cash Flow Blues

You wouldn't believe how many entrepreneurs refuse to acknowledge the importance of financial information. Some of these people are operating on the notion that a checkbook is the only thing that you need in the way of financial statements. Many entrepreneurs are running 2- or 3-million-dollar-per-year enterprises shackled with the idea that rudimentary accounting systems are enough to do the job. I knew one gentleman who was running a business with four separate departments. He didn't know which department was making or losing money. All funds were put into a soup bowl, so to speak, without being tagged to a particular department. Expenses were handled in the same manner. When this guy got into a cash flow bind he did not have anything to work with in the form of financial feedback. In addition, his accountant was incompetent, providing no advice and charging him $3600 for filling out and filing two sets of tax returns. Upon being hired as his management consultant, I immediately went to work with a CPA to straighten out the books. We were able to set up a manageable financial control system so that revenues and costs could be pegged back to the department of origin. In other words, we could track what departments were making or losing money. Control came easier after that, for obvious reasons. By the way, I fired this old accountant and recovered some previous charges. The new CPA firm charges the client less than $1000 per year to do his tax returns as well as provide accounting and financial advice as needed.

The point to learn here is really simple. If you lack the appropriate accounting and financial expertise, go get some. Take some courses at your local college or find some books discussing these topics and read them. The Small Business Administration also has some excellent publications concerning financial control and management. Write or call their headquarters in Washington, D.C., or the SBA field offices, which are usually located in the state capitals. They will send you an order form. In addition, I suggest that you find an accounting firm that offers services in the form of providing monthly financial statements. This way you can have updated financial information on a regular basis. If difficulties crop up, at least you will know that trouble exists before much damage ensues. The charge is surprisingly inexpensive, normally ranging anywhere between $60 and $120 per month. This is a truly small sum when you consider the potential rewards in terms of financial control and containment.

What you have to watch at this point is the accounting firm. Make sure that they have experience with entrepreneurial enterprises. Ask around about their reputation. Don't ask for references, because they will give you their personal friends and most satisfied clients. Find out for yourself who they serve and then seek those firms out for comment.

Diversify and Survive

Flexibility is a must in this economy. With entrepreneurial competition being what it is today you will soon learn the need to diversify into new product or service areas on a regular basis. This is even more true of enterprises that possess only one product or are trying to penetrate but a single market.

Why this situation? Technology is the villain here. It has a tremendous impact on society in terms of buying motives and perceptions. Simply put, advancing technology will replace your existing products or services in the marketplace. Of course, this is called obsolescence. However, the pace has quickened for two reasons. Technology is moving forward at an extremely fast pace, and heavy competition is shortening the life cycles of new products and services.

Now, diversification will reduce your risks in the marketplace, but it's not really that simple. You must have the right frame of mind and the willingness to move, because diversifying can be difficult. A *Wall Street Journal* article quoted one entrepreneur as saying, "You don't realize how inflexible you are until you try to diversify." The article went on to question this entrepreneur about companies who fail to diversify. He responded, "In a very short time they are going to trail off into the sunset."

In addition, careful planning and analysis is essential and this process is discussed below. Simply pursuing business opportunities without proper investigation is dangerous indeed.

Expand Upon Your Base

You should always be ready to move when expansion opportunities come knocking. Below are some tips that may help you identify new potentials.

1) Always be on the lookout for new products or services. Seize upon those that offer promise. Only through product or service diversification can you lessen your risks in the marketplace, lower per unit costs, and enhance long-term profits.

2) Identify products or services that complement your existing lines. Sell these as supplements and watch your profits grow. For example, many small newsletter publishing companies do not make money by selling the newsletter alone. The big bucks are generated by the sale of supplementary materials such as books and reports.

3) Become a primary source. Instead of distributing a product or service for someone else, investigate the possibility of primary generation. Develop the product or service yourself. You then can control the product or service, sell to other middlemen, reduce your

price, enhance your profits, etc. In other words, you are in the driver's seat and not subject to the manipulations of vendors.

4) Expanding the distribution patterns for your products and services will broaden your profit opportunities. This brings to mind a fellow who was selling financial planning services to individuals. He decided that it was time to make it big or throw in the towel. This guy approached big corporations with the idea of offering his financial planning services to their employees as a fringe benefit. He argued that it would help the employees manage their income more effectively. It worked and today he's a millionnaire.

5) Enhancing the quality of your product or service will pay, especially in today's economy. Quality sells, and all companies, large and small, are searching for the right formulas. The trick is to make sure that the price of quality enhancement does not exceed expected returns. Usually that won't happen anyway. I know this veterinarian who has always strived to maintain a quality approach to animal care. Now, I have found him to be no more effective than any other good vet. However, his quality image allows him to charge up to 75 percent more than other vets in the town. He will even investigate the fee structure of other veterinarians, and if he finds any of them charging more for their services than he gets, this guy simply raises his fees higher than theirs and proudly proclaims that he is the best vet around.

This reminds me of another interesting illustration. While in college I worked in a liquor store. One day it was brought to my attention that two different bottles of spirits were made by the same distiller. Nothing wrong with that, right? Well, it just so happened that both bottles also came from the same plant and even out of the same vat mixture. The number codes on the bottom of the bottles showed this to be true. One sold at a premium for $10.95 and the other was marketed as a middle-line product for $6.95. It was really the same product, but perception made the difference in price.

Opportunities Galore

New products or services are your profit opportunities of the future just as your current products or services generate today's revenues. All companies, both large and small, fall victim to the product/service life cycle which is shown in Table 8 on page 143 and discussed later in the book. It basically illustrates that products and services come and go. This underscores the need for your company to be constantly on the lookout for new opportunities. If you refuse to accept this business fact of life, your enterprise will not survive to see the future.

Now, you must be consistently planning for the future in terms of new products or services. And even though there are risks involved in this process, it is a must in order to ensure the future of your entrepreneurial endeavors. You can look at it another way. New products or services will help your competitive posture in the marketplace and assist in future profit generation by replacing the old and less profitable lines.

Development of a new product or service should be given much consideration. After all, much is at stake. In business there are no guarantees of success, and hitting on the right idea by accident is usually the exception and not the norm.

The First Steps

Don't jump head first into an expensive and full-blown new product or service analysis until you take a few initial steps that could save thousands of dollars in research costs. Do some preliminary investigating of your own. Table 4 will help you to forecast sales of a new business venture in a very simple and inexpensive way. Also, Table 4 identifies some sources of information that may assist you in making some up-front conclusions. You might even consider the services offered by the Wisconsin Innovation Service Center at the University of Wisconsin in Whitewater. This organization will rate your product or service based on 33 different factors. After the analysis they will forward you a detailed report, and there is only a $100 fee for this service as last reported. Cheap indeed, when you consider what you get in terms of decision-making data.

If the incoming information at this point is negative, stop all further investigation immediately. In other words, cut your losses and run. It's the mark of a good investor. Conversely, if you're receiving positive feedback, the next step is to proceed to full-scale investigation. Appendix A contains a comprehensive discussion of new product/service development. It is provided courtesy of the U. S. Small Business Administration, Guide No. 39, written by Robert W. James and entitled, *Decision Points in Developing New Products.*

TABLE 4

MAJOR WAYS OF FORECASTING SALES
OF A NEW BUSINESS VENTURE

Project sales on the basis of key market factors. First identify factors
that have affected your sales in the past and may also do so in the future.
Then estimate the impact of these factors on sales for the new venture.
When there are different projections for the future, you can do one of
two things. You can establish *probabilities* (including the relative
frequencies) of each occurring. Or, you can *rank* each of the events in
order of their likelihood of taking place. Ranking possible outcomes is
the simpler approach, but generally is less accurate than establishing
probabilities.

Survey buyer intentions. You can ask potential customers if they would
utilize your new or expanded service, and if so, how frequently.
However, keep in mind that it is best to use this information as an
indication of how good the growth potential of the new venture will be,
rather than to forecast sales. It's not likely that you'll be able to develop
the right type of survey data to obtain an accurate sales forecast—unless
you have considerable experience in conducting market research.

*Plot past sales on a graph to obtain an indication of what future sales
trends for your business will be once you have expanded.* To use this
approach effectively, you must be able to anticipate market and business
changes that can be expected to occur. The advantage of the approach is
it is simple, and you can utilize information already available to you.
The principal disadvantage is your findings are tied to past performance, which may not be a good indicator of future events.

Query a cross section of your sales representatives for their opinions.
This approach may or may not be a good one. It will work only if sales
people are of a high caliber.

Use your own judgment. This technique is best used in conjunction with
one or more of the previously mentioned sales forecasting techniques.
However, be sure not to overlook it.

Before you act, ask others for their opinions of what sales levels you
can expect from a new venture. People to talk with include other
managers of similar small service firms, suppliers, trade association
representatives, and perhaps consultants.

TABLE 4 (continued)

WARNING: If you get into a discussion with your competition, be sure
you don't enter into a situation in which you could become involved in
sales collusion. This is illegal.

Source: U. S. Small Business Administration.

Excellence Pays Dividends

Enough has been said about excellence recently to last a century, but
listen just one more time.

Consumers are becoming increasingly quality conscious once again.
They are unimpressed by the cheap alternative that is second-rate and
produced in a slip-shod way. Many companies, both large and small,
are taking the hint. You should also apply some quality control
standards to your product or service. Constant improvement is necessary in order to stay ahead of the competition nowadays. You may be
thinking that since your enterprise is a small operation a quality control
program is not affordable in terms of money and/or time. However,
even a simple program can produce tremendous feedback in terms of
improvement suggestions. In other words, ask your customers for
input and ideas.

Also, you will need to impress upon your employees the need to
excel. If given the right combination of reason and incentive, your
employees will go out of their way to make you and the customers
happy in terms of quality and service. Employee motivation is
discussed more in detail later in the book.

I will close this section of the chapter by quoting John W. Gardner,
former Secretary of the U. S. Department of Health, Education and
Welfare:

An excellent plumber is infinitely more admirable than an incompetent
philosopher. The society which scorns excellence in plumbing because
plumbing is a humble activity, and tolerates shoddiness in philosophy
because it is an exalted activity, will have neither good plumbing nor
good philosophy. Neither its pipes nor its theories will hold water.

Enhancing Your Productivity*

Executives who own or manage smaller companies in America today face a special demand as to their own management productivity.

If they make the right decisions, their companies will weather the current economic storm and be well-prepared to prosper when the economic seas return to normal.

If they don't make the right moves their companies will sink.

Most of the time, when the president of a smaller business thinks about "productivity," his mind runs to "How can I get the plant to be more efficient?" or "How can I get my people to be more productive?"

One often overlooked fact is that the president himself is potentially the most productive person in the company. What should he be doing to increase his own productivity as well as that of the staff?

Here are some guidelines to management productivity that every small business executive should follow:

1. SET CLEAR PROFIT OBJECTIVES

   You must plan specific profit flow within your company, then translate those goals into specific tasks for your key people.

2. WRITE DOWN A "CHECKLIST OF KEY PROJECTS"

   Determine which ones *only you* as president can do. Write them on a special "things for me to do" list.
   Next, determine which key people are best equipped (beyond yourself) to be responsible for the other tasks, then DELEGATE. Don't be afraid to DELEGATE. Force yourself to DELEGATE.

3. ESTABLISH REALISTIC SALES GOALS

   Do not operate with "blue sky" in your sales forecasts, no matter how persuasive or enthusiastic your sales manager might be.

4. BUILD AWARENESS ABOUT PRODUCTIVITY throughout your company.

   Do personal follow-ups on matters that pertain to productivity...
   • Efforts to increase cash flow

*This section is provided by permission of the George S. May International Company, a consulting firm specializing in small and medium-sized businesses. They are located at 111 South Washington Street, Park Ridge, IL 60068.

- Disciplining inventory control
- Eliminating wasteful activities
- Speeding up billing, slowing down payables
- Completing projects on time.

Handwritten notes from you as president to key people, or a short personal phone call about a productivity matter will be extremely helpful.

5. DEMONSTRATE "HUMAN SENSITIVITY"
    - Motivate and lead in the face of today's economic pressure. Show your staff a calm professional leadership. Don't panic and try to motivate by threatening.
    - Be honest with your employees. Share your concerns about productivity with them.
    - Emphasize a "May I help you"..."How can I help you" attitude.
    - Let employees know you want their ideas about productivity.

6. EXPLORE NEW IDEAS, NEW TECHNOLOGY that can really fit your business.
    - Affordable automation.
    - Tailor-made computerization (possibly on a time-sharing basis, without the need for a major capital outlay).
    - Telemarketing.
    - Look for new customer needs caused by today's economy; i.e., energy savings, ways to extend equipment life, new uses for slag or scrap.

7. WATCH ALL EXPENSES CLOSELY
    - Let the staff know their president is personally spot checking expenses.
    - Reject some expense statements you would have "let slide by" in better times. Be sure the staff hears about the rejection.

8. REDUCE UNPRODUCTIVE MEETINGS
    - Make each meeting justify itself with some sort of productivity enhancing decision.

9. PURGE YOUR LINES OF SLOW MOVING ITEMS
    - Weed out products that generate substandard profits.
    - Use these "tough times" to replace and upgrade marginal or disruptive people on your staff.

10. DON'T DUPLICATE EFFORT
    - Concentrate on one task at a time.

- Find and eliminate bottlenecks (even if it's your brother-in-law).
- Have each of your key people check their departments to eliminate duplication of effort...
- Look for two tasks that can be combined into one and do it.
- Identify one or more functions or reports that are not really essential and do away with them.

Be sure that you are constantly giving your staff signals—both overt and covert, verbal and non-verbal—that productivity improvement is essential—essential to survival in the short-run, critically important to job security and prosperity in the long run.

Management Imperfection

All entrepreneurs should take stock of themselves. What do I mean by this? Simply evaluate yourself on a regular and a systematic basis. In other words, make sure you are managing wisely. To do less is costly in terms of revenues and profits. How does an entrepreneur evaluate himself/herself? You conduct an audit. That's right, a management audit. It's the equivalent of the IRS looking over your income and deductions. However, in this case, you are the agent in charge of making yourself operate more effectively.

The Small Business Administration (SBA) published four booklets about how to use a management audit. Each booklet is designed for a specific type of enterprise. Write or call the Management Assistance Division of the SBA in Washington, D.C., or in your state capital and inquire about these publications. The titles are:

— Management Audit For Small Construction Firms—Series No. 40
— Management Audit for Small Manufacturers—Series No. 29
— Management Audit for Small Retailers—Series No. 31
— Management Audit for Small Service Firms—Series No. 38

The Question of Waste*

Below are 233 soul-searching questions that you may want to ask yourself. Some will not apply to your particular situation. Obviously,

*This section is provided by permission of the George S. May International Company, a consulting firm specializing in small and medium-sized businesses. They are located at 111 South Washington Street, Park Ridge, IL 60068.

an increasingly larger number of questions will apply as your entrepreneurial operation expands. Even if you are just thinking about the prospects of entrepreneurship, or your company is in its early stages, it would be wise to review these questions in order to get a leg up on problems that will most definitely ensue.

1. Administrative Controls Over Waste

(1) Do you have an organization chart: (a) Prepared how long ago? (b) Is someone responsible for keeping it up to date? (c) Is it up to date now?

(2) Is there a straight flow of authority in your organization setup? (a) Any conflict or overlapping of authority? (b) In the case of each executive, does the attendant responsibility accompany the authority granted?

(3) Do you have a written manual for each executive detailing specific duties and responsibilities? (a) Do such manuals include a clear delineation of all company policies and procedures which can be set forth in definite terms? (b) Who is responsible for keeping these manuals up to date? (c) Are they up to date now?

(4) Do you have a well-worked-out plan for understudies? (a) For major executives? (b) For minor executives? (c) Any system of promotion from the ranks? (d) Any methods of study and tests to determine eligibility for promotion?

(5) Do you have personnel records? (a) Are they kept up to date? (b) Are they complete enough as to quality and quantity of performance?

(6) Do you have a complete, modern cost and accounting system? (a) Are costs broken down for each department? (b) For each operation or assembly? (c) Are department heads held responsible for costs in their departments? (d) How long since your cost and accounting system has been scientifically analyzed and brought up to date?

(7) Are costs estimated for each department and operating unit? (a) Is responsibility fixed for keeping actual costs within estimated costs, by each department or operating unit?

(8) Do you have adequate operating reports to enable you to plan on a sound basis and quickly observe and check excessive costs? (a) Monthly budget comparison covering expense, production, labor, and plant and equipment? (b) Reports of weekly results? (c) Reports of plant activity? (d) Production labor and burden? (e) Reports of inventory? (f) Do you know the costs of production; manufacturing; labor—both direct and indirect; raw materials, supplies, and small tools; inspection; departments; stores? (g) Are you aware of dollars lost through idle machines, idle employees, machine repairs, and spoilage? (h) Do you know the actual costs vs. estimated costs?

(9) How long since all records and forms were checked for simplification and avoidance of duplication?

(10) Has office arrangement been checked recently for best flow?

(11) Do you have supervisory incentives for executives and key employees based on proper individual performance?

(12) Is your research department adequate? (a) For present needs? (b) For future planning?

(13) Have you checked employment procedure recently? (a) Adequate tests to determine employee's best capabilities? (b) Have you a definite training program for new employees? (c) Are variances supplied by upgrading as much as possible, so as to fill lowest positions with new employees?

(14) Any systematic record kept showing tabulated causes of employees leaving, discharged or laid off? (a) Have you analyzed as to causes under your control? (b) Before discharging, is any effort made to test employee's ability for other work?

(15) Have you analyzed temporary shutdowns as to how adequate controls might have prevented them? (a) Labor trouble (Wage Incentives)? (b) Unbalanced production (Production and Materials Control)? (c) Breakdowns (Preventive Maintenance)? (d) Lack of planning (Administrative Controls)?

(16) What was labor turnover for last year? (a) How does it compare with comparable industries in your area? (b) What percentage of new employees make good? (c) Have you studied effect of labor turnover on production and cost?

(17) Have you a wage incentive plan based on fair and sound standards?

(18) How much waste in productive time during last year due to strikes and lockouts?

(19) How many accidents during last year? (a) What was the cost per year as a result of such accidents (Compensation insurance and damages awarded, wages paid during incapacity)? (b) What percentage might have been prevented by adequate safety measures? (c) Anyone specifically responsible for safety control?

(20) How adequate is the company's welfare work? (a) Locker facilities, conveniently placed? (b) Toilet facilities, conveniently placed? (c) Convenient restaurant or lunch facilities? (d) Rest rooms? (e) Rest periods? (f) Recreation facilities? (g) Transportation facilities? (h) Housing conditions?

(21) Do you have a planned method of encouraging workers to make suggestions and rewards for adopted suggestions?

(22) Do you have tabulated record of time lost by employees due to ill health? (a) Cost of such lost time? (b) Analysis of unhealthy conditions?

(23) Are authority and responsibility placed in one person for all purchases? (a) Maximum and minimum stocks properly determined? (b) Closely coordinated with production schedule and accurate estimate data? (c) Quality and grade of material properly controlled by adequate specifications? (d) Material adequately inspected and tested on receipt? (e) Methods of coordination and control between purchasing and planning heads as to sufficient time for obtaining materials needed? (f) Proper follow-up on time delivery? (g) Sufficient turnover in material? (h) Comparative loss in "dead stock" over period of last three years?

(24) What methods do you have for enlisting active interest and encouraging suggestions from department heads, superintendents and foremen?

2. Waste of Space

(1) Are you utilizing plant space to best advantage?

(2) Have you had a plant layout made? (a) How recently? (b) Does it show in detail all departments, machines and work areas? (c) Any backtracking or crisscrossing in flow of work? (d) Is material storage located most strategically? (e) Is space going to waste on pillars and upper air area which could be utilized for space-saving arrangements? (f) What responsibility is delegated for continuing study of plant layout? (g) Have you held any staff meetings for suggestions of better plant layout? (h) How recently?

(3) Who is responsible for plant housekeeping? (a) Are aisles kept clear?

(4) Could you use blank side of machines for banks of material, thus better utilizing space to gain accessibility and eliminating excess handling?

3. Wastes of Productive Time

(1) Are skilled workmen required to do jobs which could be performed by less expensive labor? (a) Grinding and sharpening of tools? (b) Machine setups?

(2) Are tables and charts posted conveniently for quick reference?

(3) Is time lost deciphering poorly prepared and/or incomplete instructions?

(4) How much productive time is lost due to: (a) Waiting for materials? (b) Waiting for parts? (c) Waiting for tools?

(5) What is the cost of idle time due to inconvenient lockers, toilets, drinking fountains, eating facilities?

(6) Have you had a scientific time and motion study made of workers' operations? (a) How recently? (b) Have you increased production per man-hour this year over last?

(7) Have individual and department performance standards been determined? (a) On scientific and equitable basis?

(8) Is productive time of workers properly controlled?

(9) Have machine capacities been determined and recorded? (a) Are machines being worked to capacity? (b) Could capacities of any individual machines be increased by minor adjustments or alterations?

(10) Have you had an analysis made of grouping machines for the needs of the product to cut time between operations?

(11) Have you charts and sheets detailing operations, sequence of operations and specifying equipment to be used? (a) Are alternatives indicated? (b) Standard instructions for each operator?

(12) How is machine or work place capacity controlled?

(13) Have you a well-systematized method of continuously scheduling and recording work ahead of department, work area and worker, to prevent idle time and coordinate needs in material, tools and facilities?

(14) Is downtime of machines excessive?

(15) Do you have a continuous recording of wasted machine time? (a) Any effort to sell waste machine time?

(16) Could waste time between operations be cut down by better transportation facilities within plant?

(17) Have you analyzed material storage conditions, raw materials, processed material, finished parts and products which may cause wastes of time? (a) Better location, nearer production? (b) Excess handling? (c) Easily moved? (d) Properly indexed for ease of finding? (e) Authority fixed for issue of material? (f) Movement of material to work place properly timed and controlled?

(18) Any waste of time caused by lack of inspection? (a) Inspection after every operation where salvage could be effected and processing time saved? (b) Have you adequate methods of reporting wastes of machine and man-hours applied to parts or assemblies later rejected?

(19) Do you have adequate system of preventive maintenance? (a) Responsibility fixed? (b) Periodic inspection and repair? (c) Properly reported? (d) Machine and man-hours lost by breakdowns and repairs?

(20) Adequate tool control: (a) Responsibility fixed? (b) Analysis for possible time loss through inadequate tool control? (c) Tool room equipped properly? (d) Tool room kept neat and orderly? (e) Tools kept properly sharpened? (f) Tools standardized? (g) Department for making tools and jigs? (h) Tools assigned to work areas properly? (i) Record of tools available?

(21) Adequate designing and engineering department? (a) Are company secrets, plans and specifications of product well recorded? (b) Complete drawings of all products? (c) Complete material lists of all products? (d) Could parts going into manufacture be better standard-

ized? (e) Could odd shapes and sizes be eliminated? (f) Products of slight variation which could be standardized as to materials and processing? (g) Better interchangeability of manufactured parts?

(22) Could various operations be better standardized? (a) As to work methods? (b) Arrangement of work areas? (c) Motion sequences?

(23) Have you analyzed new timesaving technological developments for feasible application to your manufacturing operations?—e.g., infrared lamps for drying of paint and other purposes.

(24) What is your total estimated waste due to: (a) Idle time of workers? (b) Idle time of machines? (c) Deliberate curtailment of production? (d) Other factors enumerated in this section?

4. Waste of Productive Energy

(1) Have you had a scientific study made of workers' methods; (a) To eliminate unnecessarily tiring motions and fatiguing routine? (b) To provide adequate facilities to save workers' energy? (c) To prevent excess bending and motion due to poor arrangement of material and parts boxes? (d) To determine whether travelling belts or automatic conveyances save workers' energy?

(2) Adequate tests for physical condition to stand tiring and fatiguing operations? (a) To determine emotional adjustment to requirements of job?

(3) Any dust or fumes which sap workers' energy?

(4) Inadequate light causing strain?

(5) Inadequate ventilation?

(6) Insufficient rest periods?

(7) Inharmonious working conditions? (a) Thoughtless actions and attitudes of foremen?

(8) Badly functioning machines or tools?

(9) False economy in poor material?

(10) Unnecessary noise?

(11) Undue accident hazard?

(12) Needless monotony?

(13) Waste of energy on line shafts?

(14) Are motors of right capacity for load assigned?

5. Waste of Materials

(1) Adequate reports of scrap and rejects? (a) Fullest possible salvage? (b) Determination of causes? (c) Responsibility properly fixed?

(2) Waste in material due to improper storage?

(3) Waste due to excessive cuts? (a) Oversize stock used?

(4) Waste caused by poor workmanship?

(5) Waste due to poor handling methods?

(6) Waste resulting from poor condition of machines, tools and equipment?

(7) Waste caused by overloading of machines?

(8) Waste due to working to unnecessarily close limits and tolerances?

(9) Waste resulting from poor training methods?

(10) Waste due to poor inspection? (a) Inspectors capable? (b) Inspection of raw material? (c) Proper inspection standards? (d) Specifications of limits and tolerances?

(11) Centralization of authority and responsibility over quality and workmanship?

6. Waste of Technology

(1) Has computerization brought economies to your business which outweigh its cost?

(2) Does your management information system deliver data you need, when you need it, to make crucial business decisions, or does it give you so much detailed information that you fail to see the problem clearly?

(3) How many times is the same information repetitively entered into your computer for different purposes?

(4) How much productive time is wasted by your management people avoiding a cumbersome system they do not understand?

(5) How much productivity have you lost by failure to move forward into computerization, by "overshopping" for the right management information system?

(6) What have you done to educate yourself about your company's information needs, analyzing the effectiveness of your management controls? What facility has been installed to ensure your ability to *track* the progress of your business and measure achievement against your goals?

(8) Are you sure that your management information system is effective at helping you control costs, eliminate waste, and increase profit performance, or is it just another waste factor in your operation?

In Summary

When businesses rise above the common notion that waste is an acceptable folly, when buck-passing stops and top executives are willing to put themselves, as well as their organizations, under critical examination, the potentials for business improvement are infinite. There is almost certainly a 25 percent increase in productivity forthcoming.

Time Wasters

Time is money. And the proper use of time is essential. Management consultant R. Alec MacKenzie has identified 15 time wasters that can cost you in terms of lost productivity and profits. They are listed below. As an entrepreneur you must deal with them in an effective manner in order to ensure efficient operations.

1. Telephone interruptions.
2. Visitors dropping in without appointments.
3. Meetings, both scheduled and unscheduled.
4. Crisis situations for which no plans were provided.
5. Lack of objectives, priorities, and deadlines.
6. Cluttered desk and personal disorganization.
7. Involvement in routine and detail that should be delegated to others.
8. Attempting too much at once and underestimating the time it takes to do it.
9. Failure to set up clear lines of responsibility and authority.
10. Inadequate, inaccurate, or delayed information from others.
11. Indecision and procrastination.
12. Lack of or unclear communication instruction.
13. Inability to say no.
14. Lack of standards and progress reports that enable a company manager to keep track of developments.
15. Fatigue.

The three leading time wasters, according to MacKenzie, are telephone interruptions, unanticipated visitors, and meetings.

Franchising Pitfalls

Franchising is coming back in a big way. Many individuals are buying into franchises as a way to experiment with entrepreneurship. If you are lucky enough and have the money to tag a really good franchise, success is almost guaranteed. However, these franchisers may required hundreds of thousands of dollars before they will even look at you. Anyway, I'm not so sure that people who have enough money to buy into sure deals are really risk takers. For example, some would argue that calling a McDonald's franchise owner an en-

trepreneur would be like calling Fidel Castro a believer in free enterprise.

Most individuals, however, must resort to purchasing less expensive and more risky franchise operations. In addition, franchise abuse is still a problem in this country, where unscrupulous franchise organizations take advantage of unsuspecting franchisees. The point to be made here is clear. Always have your attorney look over any franchise contract that you are about to sign. Make sure that it is your lawyer who examines the contract and not the one representing the franchise organization. Also, seek out comments from some franchisees that are already connected with the organization in question. Don't rely on their references either. They will only give you the best ones. A good attorney should also inform you as to your franchise contract rights in terms of advertising support, marketing studies, training, etc.

Watch That Price

If you are thinking about buying an existing operation please be careful. In my experience as a management consultant, I would say that at least 90 percent of all acquisition price tags are too high and that in 85 percent of the cases something is seriously wrong with the enterprise up for sale. There are many methods used to find the "right" price and also to identify the firm's weaknesses. Many books have been written about them and I advise you to search them out. In addition, always have a CPA and/or management consultant review the prospective venture and even negotiate for you. Believe me, it scares the hell out of the sellers. After these guys tell you that the real worth of the acquisition is only 75 percent of the asking price, your negotiating position is much stronger. I have seen some sellers reduce their price 40 percent or more when the potential buyers have brought in their experts.

Silvester & Associates represented a couple interested in purchasing a small retail establishment. The asking price was $185,000. We valued the business at $130,000 and got the sellers to agree on a $120,000 purchase price. In addition, the buyer got a two-year lease with an option to purchase at $120,000 with all lease payments being used to reduce the price. In other words, they can purchase the business for less than $100,000. The lease will provide them with a trial run, so to speak. If they find that entrepreneurship is not for them, the agreement allows an easy out.

The contract also included a clause that disallowed the seller from competing against the new owners. Of course, this should be part of any purchase contract. You would not believe the number of sellers who come back to haunt the buyers. Recently, a Virginia entrepreneur purchased a $2.5 million restaurant and motel. Because there was no non-compete agreement, the seller is now attempting to build a new restaurant-motel across the street from the one he just sold.

It's worth the $500 or so to bring in some expert opinion when you consider what is at stake in terms of paying too much for an acquisition.

Know When to Go

Many venture capitalists will force founding entrepreneurs out of their businesses after a certain period of time. The thinking is sometimes logical. Oftentimes entrepreneurs are not very good managers. Many are excellent dreamers and doers, but when it comes to organization they fall flat on their faces. After reaching a certain stage of growth, the enterprise will need some organizational structure. In other situations some entrepreneurs just lose interest in the business.

If this is the case with you, it may be time to sell out. Start looking around for new interests or other territories to conquer.

Where to Look for Help

Table 5 lists some organizations that could provide you with a broad spectrum of assistance. Use them if you are still in doubt.

TABLE 5

OUTSIDE SOURCES OF INFORMATION

ECONOMIC

General
Chamber of Commerce
Business friends
Social friends
Advisory board
Local service clubs
Customers
Advertising, sales
Board of Directors
Newspapers
Competition—unknown

TECHNOLOGICAL		POLITICAL
Professional		*Educational and*
Services		*Governmental*
Accountants	COMPANY	Universities
Lawyers		Private and public libraries
Technical consultants	*Internal*	Small Business Administration
Management consultants		U.S. Department of
Advertising agency	Owner-manager	Commerce
Insurance	Key subordinates	Department of Agriculture
Bankers	Employees	Other Federal, State,
Investment bankers		and local agencies

SOCIAL

Trade

Trade associations
Suppliers
Professional journals
Competition—known

Source: U. S. Small Business Administration.

Chapter XII

The Imperial Customer

The Customer Is King

An important factor that stands out very clear when you are analyzing entrepreneurial success is the emphasis placed on "customer sensitivity." When asked about his business accomplishments, Mr. Jonathan Smith, the owner of the Honda auto dealership who is mentioned elsewhere in the book, said, "We have always operated on the premise that a long-time satisfied customer will do more to build your business than anything." This fact was further borne out by a recent article in *Success* magazine. Upon reviewing the many elements that contribute to small business success, the one cited in the article as being the most important was "closeness to the customer." In other words, it would seem that successful entrepreneurs know who butters their bread. In fact, customer empathy is the one area where small firms can successfully compete with the larger companies. Big corporations normally have a price advantage over their small competitors, but because of their bureaucratic nature they are substantially displaced from their customers. Smaller enterprises, who can immediately identify with their customers, have the opportunity to empathize with their clientele, which significantly counters the competitive price difference mentioned above. This factor explains why many small firms can successfully compete against large companies selling the same products or services.

To illustrate, several years ago I was in the market for a rather complicated 35mm camera. My search took me to a discount store which was part of a large regional chain. The young lady who was working behind the counter, probably for minimum wage, was no more familiar with 35mm cameras than the man in the moon. She could not answer one technical question about the photo equipment. After experiencing the same conditions at other discount stores, I paid an additional $65 premium and purchased the equipment and accessories at the local camera shop. The owner was well versed in all the technical aspects of his product. He told me that if I had any problems with the equipment to give him a call or stop back in for a refresher.

Big companies realize the importance of "customer empathy." They have been trying to get closer to their markets as of late. For example, IBM proudly proclaims that all of its employees, from top officers down to clerical personnel, are salespersons. Some of these giants have adopted the "marketing concept" as their corporate theme. In other words, all corporate decisions revolve around existing and prospective customers. (Refer to Table 6.) The marketing departments within these corporations have become the most influential source of internal

TABLE 6

FACTORS THAT INFLUENCE GROWTH

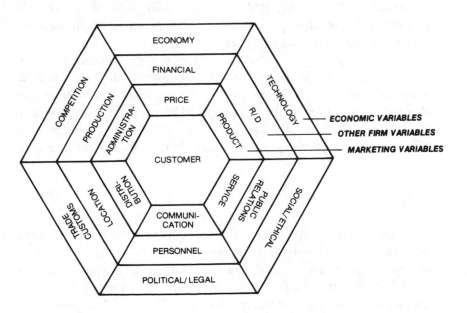

Source: U. S. Small Business Administration.

power. Sometimes they even have the power to dictate corporate goals and policies. But whatever the case, a large company will always have a tough time trying to shed its bureaucratic bias. A wall will always exist between itself (the big company) and the customer. Of course, this is an advantage for the smaller enterprise.

Now, you may think that "getting closer to the customer" is a simple process for the small business operator. Not so anymore, I'm sorry to say. The buying public is becoming increasingly fickled. Consequently, markets may change very rapidly. In addition, the previously mentioned and ever-present uncontrollable external forces could impose themselves very quickly, thereby modifying consumer tastes and preferences in short order.

Judging the Markets

Over 50 percent of the profits that your business will earn five years from now will be generated from products or services that you are not now marketing, according to the U. S. Small Business Administration. Consequently, the question becomes: Are you able to absorb a 50 percent or more reduction in revenues? Probably not. So, don't make the mistake of assuming that the future will be a repeat of past performance and that profits will be forthcoming from existing customers and marketing practices.

In an attempt to judge and exploit changes in customer behavior, various alternatives will become apparent. Don't take much time or invest a lot of money analyzing these alternatives unless you are sure there is a good probability of success. The name of the game is to locate various areas of business opportunities and to judge their commercial feasibility within a reasonable time frame and in a cost-effective manner.

Give Them What They Want

Thinking that your product or service is the best thing to come down the pike since pantyhose is a common mistake made by many entrepreneurs. Keep in mind that it is only great if your customers think it is. Nothing else really matters. Don't get me wrong here. Your opinions and the input of others, including experts, does have some relevance in the product/service selection process, but the most important thing is what the existing or prospective customers think.

Now, you can use the advice of others or information generated through your own efforts to manipulate consumer beliefs, but what ultimately matters in the buying process is what the customer is thinking and/or perceives.

The key to success in any business venture is the ability to predict what the customer will purchase. And even though buying habits can be manipulated by various stimuli, such as advertising campaigns, the best way to ensure profit fruition is to pinpoint your customer's demands and future needs. After that, you can develop or modify product/service lines in accordance with those desires. This process can entail the application of both technical and non-technical means. In other words, customer needs and desires can be identified by using formal surveys or by playing on hunches.

Technical surveys are conducted by using questionnaires to detect current needs and future desires. These questionnaires are circulated to a well defined, though limited, group of people who are supposed to be a representation and reflection of the entire market you are trying to exploit. (Market breakdown will be discussed in the next section of this chapter.) After the data on the individual questionnaires are blended and studied, a reasonable estimation of customer demands and needs can be made. Don't get the wrong idea. No procedure is foolproof. There are no guarantees that the application of scientific methods will ensure marketing success (the Edsel was proof of this). However, it might improve your odds somewhat or put you on notice that marketing mistakes are being made.

The confines of this book do not permit a discussion of the formalities of creating and using a survey questionnaire. However, Appendix B in back of the book provides you with an adequate discussion of survey methods. It is provided by permission of the American Statistical Association and is probably the best description of scientific survey methods available today. After reading the first few pages of Appendix B, don't run for the hills. It is a little technical, but I guarantee you that it will help in identifying and empathizing with your customer base. In most cases, what will emerge for entrepreneurial enterprises is a very simple survey questionnaire that is fairly straight-forward and easy to administer. For example, Table 7 illustrates a survey questionnaire that was used by a group of individuals who were developing and producing cassette tapes of Christmas music for regional distribution. This simple form provided the data they needed in order to determine whether there was a desire for the product, and

TABLE 7

QUESTIONS FOR SURVEY

1. Age:
   ____ 18-24   ____ 25-35   ____ 36-49   ____ over 50
2. Sex:
   ____ Male   ____ Female
3. Occupation: _____
   (If Student)   ____ High School   ____ College
4. What type of music do you listen to?
   ____ Classical   ____ Rock   ____ Country
   ____ Jazz   ____ Heavy Metal ____ Other _____
5. Do you like Christmas music? or are you a grinch?
   _____
6. Name two favorite Christmas songs.
   1. _____
   2. _____
7. Do you know of Shenandoah College and Conservatory?
8. Have you ever attended any performances at Shenandoah College?
   ____ Yes   ____ No
9. Would you be interested in a Christmas tape produced by Shenandoah College?
   ____ Yes   ____ No
10. What would you expect to pay for such a tape?
    $_____

the price they could demand for it. This entire survey process was completed prior to spending one cent for production and marketing costs. This product is scheduled for market introduction in October 1986.

Now we come to the non-technical aspects of determining customer wants and desires. Simply put, this amounts to playing on a hunch. It has often been said that good managers have a sixth sense which is called intuitiveness. Without a doubt, intuition is a nice managerial gift to possess and some entrepreneurs claim that most of their successes are predicated upon it. President Reagan is a perfect example. The President has made decisions based on his own hunches oftentimes in opposition to a majority of his advisors and in the face of economists who predicted that his decisions would lead our country down the path to economic demise. Guess what? A lot of economists in Washington are looking for jobs these days. Of course, I am not trying to suggest that Ronald Reagan is an entrepreneur, nor am I recommending that you should rely solely on your hunches.

What's interesting is the fact that most of the entrepreneurs that we researched for this book stated that they had not conducted any formal customer or marketing studies before initiating operations. Yet today they are successful in their own right. But what must be considered here is that for every success there are 2 to 3 failures, and I am not about to interview the failures. What's more, the U. S. Small Business Administration states that 60 percent of entrepreneurial failure is due to inadequate markets for the products and services being attempted in the marketplace. Obviously, being aware of marketing potentials through a properly conducted survey, will help reduce the chance of entrepreneurial failure.

After employing a reasonable scientific survey questionnaire to determine your customer's wants and future desires, allow your ingrained instincts to guide you the rest of the way. The "gut feelings" and "hunches" are an important aspect of the decision-making process and consequently they deserve consideration. They could mean the difference between success or failure. For example, we now know that if NASA officials had played to their "gut feelings" on the morning of January 28, 1986, the space shuttle tragedy would have been pre-vented, according to investigation experts. There was apparently a sufficient body of suspicion to suggest that the risk of launch was far greater than any possible rewards that could have been gained by one successful shuttle flight. Impulsiveness and ambition stood in the way of the usually safety-conscious NASA officials in charge of the shuttle program, and disaster ensued.

Another thing must be considered here. Competitiveness within the entrepreneurial ranks is growing at a feverish rate. Everybody's brother and sister is entrepreneuring. Absolute and comparative advantages in products or services will be reserved only for those companies having proprietary technology in their possession. And that doesn't usually last very long. In other words, competition is the name of the game and it's only going to get worse. Now, excessive competition should not scare you. Although, in order to thrive in the marketplace you must do somewhat better than your competition. This might entail lower prices, more efficient service, better guarantees, more effective management in general, etc.

In my experience as a small business consultant, I have found that most prospective entrepreneurs fail to see or understand the importance of determining customer needs and future wants. They are blinded by what they perceive to be the "best product in the world." Then they move into the marketplace unaware and are surprised when sales do not ensue. You definitely gain the upper hand by knowing in advance what products or services will be marketable. This in itself will lessen the chance of failure and may prevent financial loss and the acquiring of psychological scars.

MARKET CONSIDERATIONS

Before embarking upon a survey campaign you will need to identify your market. Few entrepreneurial endeavors have the capability of selling to everybody. Many are limited by the specialized nature of their products/services and/or geographic constraints (Why sell snow tires in Miami?). In addition, lack of capital and marketing expertise could be factors that might restrict market penetration. At times, the market for a product or service is quite evident and rather general in nature. A drugstore would have as its market almost everyone, although it would probably serve a specific localized customer base.

Market identification, sometimes referred to as "segmentation," is accomplished by studying "demographic profiles." In other words, all markets can be segmented into various smaller markets. Some common demographics are listed below.

> Age
> Income
> Education
> Marital Status
> Employment Classification
> Religion
> Race
> Geographics
> Political Affiliations

For example, financial planning services have become very popular lately. Most of these services are offered on a localized basis by individual practitioners who do not have the capability to market on a national or even regional basis. Furthermore, financial planning services are not geared to every household. Evidence has shown that the primary market for this service is urban white-collar professionals who earn in excess of $30,000 per year. The large record companies have as their market the entire country, but even they limit their promotional activities to individuals under 25 years of age.

Almost every major corporation in America is moving away from generalized markets to more segmented ones. This can be observed in the recently reported shift in advertising dollars away from broadcast media to more specialized media outlets such as cable television. So you can see that it is very important to define your market in very specific terms. Only after you do this can you then query your prospective customers in order to determine sales potential.

Now we know the importance of demographics as they relate to the demand and marketing of your products and services. However, customer needs and desires are also affected by other factors as well. Prevailing opinions, media publicity and advertising, fads, and trends can all manipulate demand for your products or services. The name of the game is to pinpoint your market and keep up on those factors that cause your customers to change their attitudes and tastes. Some other considerations that you should be aware of include but are not limited to the following:

> Changes in Competitor Behavior
> Alterations in Supplier Availabilities
> Media Coverage of Your Products or Services
> Changing Views of Experts in Your Field of
>   Endeavor
> The Track Record of Your Competitors

COMPETITIVE CONSIDERATION

At this point we have determined that you need to adequately identify the segmented market to which you want to sell. In addition, you must get to know your customers and determine how your product or service appeals to their needs and desires. As stated earlier, a survey campaign can help you accomplish this task. Now you must determine why your product/service will sell in the marketplace. Is it unique? Is it more economical than your competitor's? Does it have more attractive features or is it superior in quality? Will it heighten the customer's feeling of self-worth or status?

One thing is sure, competitors cannot be ignored. To some extent, competition will determine the way you market your product or service and the price you ask for it. Ultimately competitors will also determine the particular products or services you will market. To preserve your position against competitive pressures you will need to stay on guard at all times with the objective of outflanking your competitors. Your product or service must stand out from the others in the marketplace. Of course, this requires an ever-constant review of what you're attempting to sell. Updating or modification of product or service lines may be needed periodically in order to beat the competition. If you remember, this process of evaluation was discussed in Chapter XI. Just keep in mind that every product or service goes through a "life cycle." This cycle is illustrated in Table 8 and discussed below. From a marketing standpoint, product or service profitability will depend on where it finds itself in the life cycle.

STAGES OF THE LIFE CYCLE

INTRODUCTION STAGE—This phase exists when the product or service is new and original in the eyes of the buying public. Few competitors are involved in marketing the new product or service and demand is beginning to become evident. Consequently, profit margins are attractive and the ability to carve out significant market shares is present.

GROWTH STAGE—This phase is characterized by the demand for the product or service exceeding available supply. There are not enough supplies, and profits are soaring at this point. High profits begin to attract competitors. Profits peak at the latter end of this stage.

MATURITY STAGE—This phase takes place when the demand for the product or service is in equilibrium with available supply. Prices begin to stabilize because there is an increased number of competitors in the marketplace.

DECLINE STAGE—This phase is characterized by an oversupply of products or services. Demand begins to slacken. Competition is fierce, with too many competitors in the marketplaces. Prices are falling at this point. This stage is sometimes referred to as the "shake down."

SATURATION STAGE—This phase takes place after the market shake down. Many competitors either fail or diversify out of the product or service. Equilibrium between demand and supply is again

TABLE 8

The Product Life Cycle

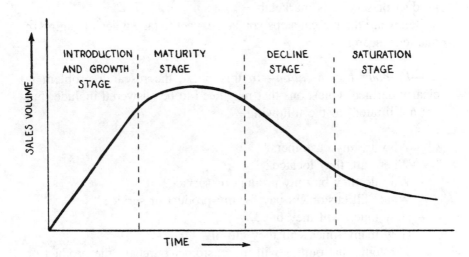

achieved, although at a lower price than before. The product or service has run its course and the market is viable only to the degree that consumers want replacements.

It may be worth noting that the "death" of a product or service can be delayed to some degree by constant modification. For example, the early electronic calculator manufacturers avoided the later stage of the life cycle by periodically adding new function keys to their calculators. In addition, some "dead" products may find rebirth in a new generation of customer. The skateboard, very popular in the mid-1960s, is today experiencing a comeback. CB radios have already gone through two life cycle experiences in a fifteen-year period.

A thorough understanding of the "life cycle" is important. Ignoring it could be disastrous to your financial health.

MARKET RESEARCH

Once you have a product or service that has some merit and potential with a clearly defined market, your next step is to conduct some further studies. Market research is much like problem resolution in that you are trying to find the answer to some important questions. This process is very critical to entrepreneurial success because it provides answers and data about the buying habits and motivations of your customers. These answers may be multifold, given the fact that you're trying to make complex determinations as to whether your product or service is marketable.

Below are the typical steps you can expect to take when engaging in market research.

—*Problem Identification*—In this phase the research problem is clearly defined. Questions that may need to be answered include, but are not limited, to the following:

—Who are my customers?
—Where are they located?
—Why do they buy my product or service?
—What will customers pay for my product or service?
—How much will they buy?
—How many times will they buy it?
—Through what outlets will my customer purchase the product or service?
—Who are my competitors?
—What advertising media should be used?

This list could go on forever. The questions that need to be answered really depend on the product or service being marketed. Each will demand its own set of questions.

—*Initial Investigation*—This phase attempts to put the research problem into clearer focus. Secondary (existing) sources of data are examined and experts in the field are queried for their opinions. Trade associations are primary depositories of helpful information.

—*Research Planning*—At this point you know what facts must be unearthed. And you should be aware of how they will be obtained. Primary research (original surveys and forecasts) will be used interchangeably with secondary data in order to reach a decision.

—*Data Pursuit*—Once the plan is delineated you can begin to collect the information. The choice of collection procedure depends on the plan and information available. It may entail telephone or mail surveys as well as personal interviews.

—*Data Assimilation*—After the data are collected, they must be interpreted and absorbed so as to assist in the decision-making function. This is also the phase where unscientific inputs, such as "hunches" and "gut feelings," may enter into the process.

—*Conclusion*—Once both scientific and unscientific data have been interpreted, it is now possible to reach a conclusion. However, if the research process or the input data is flawed or insufficient, this reality must be reflected in the decision process.

MARKET TESTING

The real litmus test as to the worth of your products or services is the marketplace's reaction to them. But before committing large amounts of time and money to prove their marketability, you may want to conduct a test-marketing campaign. Simply put, it allows you to "test the waters" in a small way. This will give you the opportunity to assess the market potential of your wares. For example, a restaurant owner may want to supplement his/her menu even though the present food selection is adequate and profitable. Of course, the objective is to generate additional sales or to find new customers. Whatever the case, before a menu modification is permanently adopted, the change should be tested for a short period of time to determine its acceptability to existing and new customers. If the change is not well received, a reversal can be executed without much difficulty or loss of time and money.

The important point to remember here is that your customers must be aware of the efforts to implement change. You must make an attempt to educate your existing and prospective customers. Without doing this a market test would be impossible.

TRIAL AND ERROR

As was stated earlier, all of the entrepreneurs that were researched for this book indicated that they did not conduct a marketing survey prior to going into business for themselves. Consequently, this book has outlined the risks of doing nothing to ensure a market for your product or service.

In reality, most entrepreneurs rely mostly on trial and error as a decision-making technique. Given the fact, as officially published by Dun & Bradstreet, that approximately 60 percent of all entrepreneurial failures are due to an inadequate market for products and services, relying solely on the trial-and-error method reminds me of the old Fram Oil Filter commercial on television. The message was clear— pay a little now or a whole lot later. In other words, the small investment input for a marketing survey and test program may more than offset the loss incurred due to a full-blown marketing campaign that failed. The trial-and-error method may be too costly in terms of losses incurred before rewards are achieved.

The above is not to suggest that surveying and/or testing will ensure success. On the contrary, there are no guarantees, but it does reduce the risk.

Is It Feasible?

It is not enough to have the best product or service in the world. Even if everyone beats a path to your door, it doesn't make sense to sell it unless markets can be penetrated at a profit. Herein lies a problem of great proportion. Many prospective entrepreneurs are impulsive and quick to take action without engaging in a comprehensive investigation. Even if your marketing studies indicate that an adequate customer base exists, you still need to conduct a profit analysis. This procedure, outlined in Appendix A, ensures to some degree that your product or service will generate an appropriate return on investment.

MARKET PROMOTION AND STRATEGY

So far we have been dealing with the particulars of customer identification, buying motivations, competition, market testing, and feasibility analysis. Once you have determined that a market exists for your product or service and that it can be exploited in a profitable manner, your next step is to delineate a marketing strategy.

Your overall marketing strategy must take into account the four P's of the marketing mix. They are:

—Product (or service)
—Price
—Promotion
—Place (also known as distribution)

These elements are interrelated and one cannot exist separately without the others. However, each has a different degree of importance depending upon what product or service you are attempting to sell and/or the stage of the life cycle in which the product or service finds itself. For example, if you're selling hand-held electronic calculators, the important elements become price and place. These products are in the saturation phase of their life cycles, where competition abounds. Therefore, a good price and immediate delivery are the keys to success in marketing these units. Conversely, if you are marketing high-priced industrial equipment, the most important elements become the product itself. Price, promotion, and place take a subordinate position in this case. However, if you are attempting to sell a brand new service that is unique in the marketplace, promotion and the product itself become the most important elements. Because it is new, customers will not pay much attention to price and will even wait for delivery.

After you understand the marketing mix it will be time to develop your marketing strategy. Now, we have already discussed in detail how to determine whether there is a market for your product or service and what price you can expect to get for it. Next in line for consideration would be an evaluation of place (distribution). Your product or service will need to be distributed. How will it be done? Do you need to warehouse it? How much will it cost? Are channels of distribution needed? If so, what kind? Are salespersons needed? How much commission are you going to pay dealers, distributors, and salespersons?

After you have determined the distribution characteristics of your product or service, the next step is the development of a promotional game plan. This is really the guts of your marketing strategy. You may have the best product or service in the world, but if consumers are unaware of its existence, sales will not materialize. Herein we have a problem of immense magnitude, and that is the selection of the most productive promotional media. When evaluating various media, several things must be considered. These include audience depth, audience sensitivity, audience demographics, and cost of media.

— Audience Depth—total size of your market.
— Audience Sensitivity—the prospects within the total market who are most likely to purchase your product or service.
— Audience Demographics—the breakdown of the market into economic and/or social characteristics.

— Cost of Media—normally expressed as CPM (cost per thousand). It represents the amount of money needed to reach 1000 prospects.

When considering the appropriate media, keep in mind that the "broadcast" era is giving way to one dominated by "narrowcasting." Television and radio stations, magazines, newspapers, and other media are carving out particular audience niches. Cable television is a prime example of this movement. Today, there are nearly 30 cable television networks and most are targeting specific viewers. There are cable networks geared to the arts, female programming, personal finance, health, etc. Table 9 illustrates the importance of demographic narrowcasting.

In addition, some promotional media are more flexible than others when trying to target particular audiences. Even though newspapers are among the least costly promotional media to use, they offer the least flexibility. Consequently, it may not be the optimal way to go. On the other hand, direct mail is very costly to employ, but it offers maximum flexibility in trying to reach a certain market. In this regard, Table 10 highlights the differences between three different media.

To some degree the choice of media depends on your product or service. If it is of a general nature, then a newspaper promotion may be the most appropriate media. Conversely, a product or service with a narrow customer base may dictate more specific media approaches. Also, the characteristics of the product or service may affect media selection. For example, if the product needs to be illustrated in order to sell, you may be locked into the visual media.

It is beyond the scope of this book to examine the intricate details of marketing strategy. In fact, the purpose of this chapter is to inform you of the importance of the "customer" to entrepreneurial success. However, it is important for you to be informed of some broad concepts. I sincerely recommend that you seek out some marketing books at your nearest college library. Some of these works direct attention specifically to small business marketing. Most tend to be more helpful than available government publications.

CUSTOMER RELATIONS

Once you have mastered the art of satisfying customer needs in a profitable way, the next step is to keep what you have. In other words, make the customer happy.

TABLE 9

DEMOGRAPHICS

Age	Station A	Station B
Under 18	43%	6%
18–25	27%	7%
26–35	13%	23%
36–50	8%	42%
Over 50	9%	22%
Income		
0–$5,000	64%	5%
$ 5,001–$10,000	16%	8%
$10,001–$20,000	11%	27%
Over $20,000	9%	60%
Education		
High School Graduate	42%	12%
College Graduate	12%	65%
Graduate School	3%	23%
Occupation		
Student	51%	5%
Unemployed (non-student)	10%	1%
Clerical	7%	8%
Skilled	8%	7%
Unskilled	6%	7%
Technical	7%	27%
Managerial	6%	26%
Professional	6%	19%
Sex		
Male	46%	73%
Female	54%	27%

The audience of Station A is considerably younger, has a lower income, less education, and fewer job skills than audience B. Nevertheless, the more youthful audience A might be a higher quality audience for certain products such as records, contemporary clothing, or fast foods.

To the seller of higher priced items such as expensive automobiles, home furnishings, or real estate, audience B would be far more interesting.

Source: U.S. Small Business Administration.

TABLE 10

	AUDIENCE	MESSAGE	COST PER 1000	EXPECTED SALES RETURN
Newspaper Advertising	Large, scattered	Brief, universal	$2–$15	1%
Television Advertising	Medium, selective	Intermediate	$100–$1000	1%–10%
Personal Selling	Small known	Detailed, specific	$250/ day	10%–?

Source: U.S. Small Business Administration.

A customer relations policy is the foundation of any successful marketing endeavor. It will help you secure and build long-term sales and profits. Just remember that closeness to the customer is one of the few factors that allow entrepreneurial firms to compete successfully with larger firms that are more cost competitive in the marketplace. Teaching yourself and your employees to be "customer conscious" will go a long way toward assuring profits and survival.

Table 11 illustrates an example of a good customer-relations policy that might be developed by a small service enterprise. It has been provided courtesy of the U. S. Small Business Administration.

Why All the Fuss?

I think that the *Wall Street Journal* sums up this entire chapter by noting the following in a recent article:

Keeping an eye on the competition, of course, is a vital part of running any business. But the way it is done is changing, particularly for small businesses. Increasingly, business owners are strengthening their ties to customers in the hope of gaining insights about competitors that they can turn to their advantage. In addition, the approach (getting closer to the customer) is also spreading because the notion of strategic planning, long practiced by big U. S. companies, is percolating down to smaller

TABLE 11

- Tell your customers how to spot potential abuses in your industry and what to do about them. Don't, however, name your competitors. You don't build your image by climbing all over theirs.

- Furnish your customers with a reasonable and easily understood guarantee of your services.

- If yours is a repair business, always return replaced parts to customers along with an explanation of what was wrong.

- If the bill is going to exceed your estimate, call the customer before you spend his or her money.

- Invest part of your time in training your employees in customer relations.

- Use follow-up letters and questionnaires to thank your customers and to determine if your service has been satisfactory. Use the information you generate to correct problems.

- Develop a code of ethics for your business. Put it in writing and communicate it to your employees. Don't assume your employees know where you stand.

- Make these policies known to your customers and tell them how they can reach you if they have a complaint.

- Resolve complaints fairly and quickly. While you should "bend over backwards" to be fair, don't let yourself be victimized by consumer fraud.

- Don't be afraid to guarantee your customers fair treatment, but remember, honesty is an intangible asset. Unless you back it up with tangible evidence and results, the chances are that an "honesty" theme won't carry you. You have to show them you are honest.

Source: U.S. Small Business Administration.

concerns. Owners are taking a longer-term view of their companies and a more disciplined approach to analyzing the players in their markets.

Table 12 provides a list of organizations that can assist you in customer and marketing related matters.

TABLE 12

1. Advertising agencies.
2. Customers.
3. Direct mail firms.
4. General marketing consultants.
5. Market researchers.
6. Packaging specialists.
7. Product development consultants.
8. Sales promotion consultants.
9. Sales employment agencies.
10. Site selection specialists.
11. Suppliers.
12. Traffic and warehousing consultants.
13. Various local, state and federal agencies.

Source: U. S. Small Business Administration.

Chapter XIII

Creative Focus and Idea Generation

Entrepreneurship and the Creative Spirit

There is one thing that definitely separates the entrepreneur from the typical small business owner and that is "creative spirit." Entrepreneurs love to be creative. They strive to invent, innovate, change, experiment, and modify. Unfortunately, those entrepreneuring souls within the corporate ranks who are often faced with unappreciative bosses and jealous peers, are seldom given the chance to be creative. Many of these internal entrepreneurs, now referred to as "intrapreneurs" in the business world, are suppressed and viewed as "boat rockers." Some are pigeonholed rather than promoted.

However, many giant companies that are facing contracting markets and falling profit margins are calling upon the creative spirits of these intrapreneurs in an attempt to secure their future. The traditional small business owner is also finding the going tough. Entrepreneurial competition is growing in leaps and bounds. The "baby boomers" are starting all kinds of businesses in record numbers. Even the tiny mom and pop grocery store on the corner will need to be creative and idea-oriented in order to survive.

In essence, creativity is the process of looking at things differently. It may also entail approaching problems and decision-making in something less than a traditional way. Dr. Edward deBono, the world-renowned psychologist, shows us that it does not take an IQ of 130 to be a creative thinker. In fact, he believes that people of average intelligence can think like geniuses if they employ the right tools. A *Readers Digest* article about deBono's methods stated, "The difference between creative and dull thinking lies not so much in our mental equipment as in how we use it."

Look at the man in Georgia who invented a device capable of generating "unlimited power." The scientific community as well as the popular media agree that this guy has invented a machine that creates more energy than it uses. It draws energy from the earth's magnetic fields and converts it to electricity. Of course, this is an unlimited source of power. The trick was to tap into it, and he did. Now the U. S. Patent office will not give this gentleman a patent because his invention smacks of "perpetual motion," and according to the Patent Office a device of this nature is impossible to build. But, let's not forget that this same patent office initially refused to give the Wright Brothers patents for their new-fangled flying machines. So much for the creative insight of government bureaucrats.

Upon being queried, this simple and uneducated basement inventor implied that anyone can be creative if they put their mind to the task. He acknowledged that many of the great inventions of the last century were discovered by average people who lacked formal training.

We all have the capability to think in creative terms; however, it may take some training. More recently, our educational institutions have come under criticism for not teaching proper thinking skills. It has been said that our finest business schools are putting out executives who do not have the necessary thinking and creative abilities to deal with the increasingly complex problems of the business world. Students are taught to apply standardized methods to every problem situation. Some call this the Harvard "step" approach to problem solving, where methodical procedures are used to deal with problems.

We have an educational environment in this country dominated by an over-emphasis on lecture and by the application of inappropriate tools to classroom discussions of real-life case studies. This is leading many companies to question the value of MBAs and business graduates in approaching and solving future corporate problems. Some of these corporations required business grads to have a wider "breadth of study" background before hiring them. A few companies even prefer liberal arts graduates over business students because they perceive them to be better thinkers.

Some primary and secondary school systems are so concerned about the thinking skills of their children that they are seeking outside advice from experts in this new field. Dr. deBono, who was mentioned earlier, is one such expert. He has pioneered the concept of "lateral thinking," which has been defined as the ability to see things differently. Many school systems, colleges, and private companies have used deBono's system as well as others. Some countries, such as Venezuela, even require children to take instruction in thinking skills. Dr. deBono trained the 106,000 Venezuelan teachers to deliver such a program of study.

Before we get into a discussion of how you can apply the creative process to entrepreneurial endeavors, let's look at some interesting examples of creativity in action. During the War of 1812, American troops attempted and finally succeeded in invading portions of Canada. On one such attempt at the American-Canadian border, the British commander quickly determined that he was hopelessly outmanned and outgunned. He noticed, however, that the American general was observing his position and trying to estimate his troop strength through a clearing of trees in the woods that separated the two opposing forces. The British leader knew that he had to think or sink. He abruptly ordered his men to stand and begin marching in a circle in front of the clearing. After the British marched for half a day, the American general was convinced that he faced an enemy of vastly superior numbers and so he withdrew, only to live on in the annals of military blunders.

More recently, the Washington, D.C. police department initiated a creative plan to apprehend some criminals at large. A letter on disguised stationery was sent to the last known addresses of over 1000 people wanted on court warrants, inviting them to a party. The letter stated that those who attended the party would receive free season tickets to Washington Redskin football games. Guess what? The party generated over 100 arrests.

Another example of creative flair involved an entrepreneur who was having some trouble with his employees on Monday mornings. He was experiencing a 10 percent absentee rate. The entrepreneur decided to change the payday from Friday to Monday. Bingo! Absenteeism dropped by 60 percent and stabilized in a normal range.

It has already been stated that the creative process is not strictly reserved for geniuses. In fact, research studies have shown that most creative people do not possess an extraordinary ability that sets them apart. Anyone with average intelligence can be creative, but it does require thinking, and some people would consider that hard work.

Nobody seems to know what stimulates creative behavior. However, psychologists have identified various mental blocks that *prohibit* creative thinking. Acknowledging the existence of these blocks will help diffuse their debilitating effects.

The first block is perceptional in nature. Each individual has a particular view of the world. This perception can be influenced by any number of factors, including, but not limited to, level of education, employment background, personal objectives, and problem-solving experience.

A second barrier to creative thinking is cultural block. We are all conditioned to accept and abide by societal norms. To one degree or another, every individual is affected by the attitudes and belief systems of employers, peers, and social organization to which they belong. And all of these demand conformity to their way of thinking or doing things. This pressure to follow the crowd, which is very strong in this country, and the unwillingness to break with tradition and/or standard norms, will have an impact on the way we think and make decisions. In fact, many employers count on "conformity systems" to keep their rabble-rousing creative creatures at bay. Most organizations will tolerate a little messing around with the system, but an individual out to beat or circumvent the system in a consistent and substantial way will be labeled a "boat rocker" and "trouble maker." Many will be suppressed and some may be fired or forced to resign. Thank heavens that a few companies are beginning to see the light. In the future, economic reality will force more organizations to think creatively in order to survive.

You must recognize the cultural blocks impeding your creative thinking. Only after you successfully eliminate or deal with those blocks that are generated at home, school, work, church, or with friends, will you be able to think in creative terms.

Another block to creative thinking happens to be the traditional way in which most people solve problems. Earlier, the "step approach" was mentioned and identified as something less than creative. Without a doubt, most people tend to be "two-dimensional" in their thought processes. Thinking patterns seem to reject the notion of adding an additional element to the decision-making process, even though this would expand the list of possible solutions to a problem. For example, many American companies, both large and small, upon facing cost increases for raw materials and other resources, will either increase the price of their products/services or drop the current lines in favor of more profitable ones. Now, more creative foreign companies tend to look between the lines. Many will seek to find internal economies or cost savings in order to avoid a price increase that could adversely affect their competitive standing in the marketplace.

The point to ponder here is that in any given problem situation your number of remedial alternatives will increase as the breadth of your thinking expands. In other words, creative thinking increases your options.

Below are listed some techniques that can be applied to help you enhance your creative thinking skills. Practice them; you never know what may happen.

1) BE OPEN TO NEW IDEAS. In order to be creative you must be positive and keep an open mind to new ideas. Patience is also important, since some ideas may initially seem impractical; after careful consideration, they may take on pragmatic characteristics.

2) PROBLEM EMPATHY. You must be able to identify problems that threaten your entrepreneurial endeavors. In fact, problem identification is the most important step in the decision-making process. Unfortunately, this is the point where most entrepreneurs fail the test of good management—recognizing problems and acting to solve them. Remember the old adage, "A good manager is one who solves a problem before it becomes a problem." In other words, the problem is neutralized or minimized before it threatens profits.

3) PREP YOURSELF. Be prepared to immerse yourself in ways to defeat a problem. This process will include the collecting of detailed information and the delineation of proposed courses of action.

4) INITIATE NEW IDEAS. In this stage you attempt to generate as many new ideas as possible directed at a particular problem. A greater number of ideas will increase the probability of finding a viable solution. If you have other associates you may want to engage in a "brainstorming" session.

5) GERMINATION. Allow any new ideas the chance to germinate. Unless you're in a crisis situation, it is better to sit on an idea for a little while. Time is a good evaluator. It allows the largely unused yet powerful subconscious mind to arrange the facts. This uncontrollable instinct will discriminate among the facts and provide good feedback about idea possibilities.

6) IDEA EXPANSION. Once a creative idea has been accepted by the mental process, it is not unusual for the idea to build upon itself and therefore enhance your opportunities. However, this is a spontaneous

process that can happen at any time—while mowing the grass, riding in the car, watching television, or tending to the garden. Just remember that idea generation is not a controlled process and it can be stimulated by any number of stimuli. In order to enhance your ability to expand upon ideas, you will need to block any influences that may disrupt or distract your thinking once idea expansion takes hold. Being alert, positive, and open-minded will help. Also, any visualized expansions upon the original idea should be recorded immediately, since most thoughts that pop in and out of the mind are easily forgotten.

7) EVALUATION. Once an idea or group of ideas is accepted as a solution to a problem, it should be tested. Entrepreneurs will use either scientific methods (decision models) and/or less formal techniques (gut feelings, comments from other entrepreneurs, etc.) to accomplish this task.

New Ideas Mean Money in the Bank

This section will show you how to develop new ideas that can be applied to any entrepreneurial situation. It is most important because new ideas and product/service diversification are the keys to surviving in this highly competitive and ever-emerging entrepreneurial economy. Pay attention. Here are some techniques that can be employed to capture ideas.

1) Always record your ideas. Any thought can become fleeting in a hurry. Write it down or record it on tape. I know one inventor who does not go out without a notebook. Since an idea can pop in or out of his head at any time, he is prepared to record it for future reference and evaluation.

2) Lay back and let your mind run wild. Often the best time for idea generation is when you're relaxed or doing something enjoyable. Take 20 or 30 minutes a day and set it aside for creative thinking. It may be while you are soaking in a hot tub or jogging down the road. Whatever, just do it.

3) Always look around and question. Never take anything at face value, especially in the world of business. Poke, pry, and question everything. Question the motives and the actions of your competitors, customers, employees, suppliers, and, yes, even yourself. You do not have to question overtly, which could get you into trouble. However, there is no better stimulation to creative thinking than a question that you are unable to answer.

4) Build upon and expand the base of old ideas. The implementation of an old idea can lead to the creation of a new one. Keep in mind that many new ideas are just refinements of past ideas. Carefully evaluate old ideas with the intention of extracting new approaches.

5) An existing idea can be modified to yield a new one. Changing an idea, either adding to or subtracting from it, could yield a new solution to a problem. Redesigning the existing idea may also yield a new alternative.

6) Use brainstorming to stimulate ideas. Many companies, large and small, use this tactic to increase creativity. In this situation, you and your associates and/or advisors sit around and record ideas as they pop into your minds. Now, there are no controls here. No matter how silly an idea may sound, it should be given consideration. Some of the greatest inventions were first viewed as useless and wastes of time. The main objective here is to generate as many ideas as possible, without initially considering merit. It is felt that volume will produce a viable idea or at least a concept that can be molded into usable form.

7) Put yourself in the shoes of the other person (competitor, customer, employee, supplier, etc.) and see if your existing ideas change or new ones emerge. Experts today are telling entrepreneurs to empathize with customers and competitors in order to get a better understanding of the marketplace.

8) Take advantage of unusual circumstances. Unexpected events can provide unexpected opportunities. However, you must be flexible and willing to move quickly. For example, the recent defeat of the Socialist Party in France provides massive opportunities for those daring souls willing to venture. French francs, the Paris stock market, and the whole economy of France will benefit and once again become a haven of foreign investment. I remember one enterprising entrepreneur who said that he became wealthy by reading the newspaper and listening to the nightly news.

Chapter XIV

Rewards and Risk Taking

Risk Aversion and Failure: Country or Individual

We live in a time when people are very security conscious. Everywhere you turn individuals are seeking security in their jobs, investments, marriages, and friendships. Over the last decade many people have come to me for investment advice. You would be surprised at the number of individuals who ask if my recommendations are 100 percent guaranteed or insured somehow. Even if I suggested a Mutual Fund with a 10-year track record of paying 50 percent per annum, at least 80 percent of those seeking advice would be concerned about a guarantee. Even today, with the stock market breaking all the records and reaching new heights, the individual investor is taking a back seat to the institutional player who is increasingly accounting for more market transactions.

At various times during my professional life I've had the responsibility of making hiring decisions. Believe me, there was nothing more depressing than fielding a lot of questions about retirement benefits from recent college grads, generally no older than 22 years of age. My position was clear on this subject. One or two questions were fine. Any more indicated to me that the person asking was too "security prone" to be an effective decision-maker in a highly competitive marketplace.

Who is to blame for this type of thinking? Well, it is society in general. During the 1960s and 1970s the federal government passed gobs of social legislation that were designed to provide a "security net" for the American people and many of the country's institutions.

Transfer payments in the form of welfare guarantees, food stamps, and unemployment compensation were substantially enhanced. The Social Security system became a primary retirement program, but it was originally intended to be only a supplement to other retirement income. Personal and business bankruptcy laws were liberalized and the federal government moved to bail out financially troubled giant corporations that were both inefficient and undeserving of salvation. In addition, the government began to aggressively regulate industries and giant corporations, thus protecting their markets and profits. Likewise, organized labor was allowed to decouple wage demands from productivity, thereby contributing to inflation.

Now it was very upsetting to watch the captains of major companies and industries pleading to congressional committees that the government should protect their markets against competition. God help them if they have to compete, right? Their objectives were obvious. Competition meant that they would have to shed some of their extremes and become more lean and mean. Ineffective managers and the "good ole boy" network would be compromised. Those unable to compete based on price, efficiency, and service would cease to be viable in the marketplace. Right, Frank Borman?

Also, national taxation policies were modified and geared so that the industrial base of our country would pay for the aforementioned programs. For example, the capital gains tax was increased in the late 1960s. Almost all venture capital in the country immediately dried up, leaving many small firms and entrepreneurs without viable sources of funding until this tax was reduced in 1978 and 1981. Now, we have already discussed the tremendous contributions that the small business community makes to the economy. No wonder American productivity and real economic growth collapsed in the 1970s. Only after the devastating effects of double-digit inflation became apparent to all of us did the winds of change begin to blow. Even today, President Reagan has difficulty in restructuring programs and taxes that attempt to provide economic incentive by loosening the "security grid" in this nation.

Obviously, many people feel comfortable with some degree of security provided by the government. Herein lies a problem of great proportions. It is hard to take candy from a kid. Once you're on the dole it's hard to get off. The leaders of Australia, Great Britain, and Sweden will tell you this.

The President's Task Force on International Private Enterprise conducted a study of economic growth in developing countries. It concluded the following:

> When governments themselves take on the responsibility of intervening in economies through greater direct control and ownership, pervasive regulation of private domestic and foreign investment, and very high taxation coupled with large public expenditures, the result is usually negative. When a government allows and encourages private enterprise and investment to take place, the results have been much more positive.
>
> The conviction that economic growth is more effectively achieved when governments assume a private enterprise strategy is supported by a growing body of research. Research findings conclude that accelerated growth is achieved when the direct role of government in the economy is reduced over time. They suggest that a government's role in productive economic activity should be indirect, through policy formulation and program assistance, rather than direct, through ownership and management. The findings further indicate that reduced government expenditure, taxation, borrowing, and regulation coupled with a greater reliance on private enterprise not only result in faster growth, but also in more efficient use of resources.
>
> Pursuing a private enterprise strategy does not imply that there is no role for government. A country's government must decide initially to allow market forces to operate in the economy, encourage individual INITIATIVE to find full commercial expression, assist in creating an environment conducive to RISK-TAKING and INNOVATION, and provide the necessary infrastructure. It does suggest that government must define its policies carefully and avoid impeding private sector growth.

Let's take a look at the Soviet Union for a moment. Here is a country that is three times the size of the United States. It has a greater number of natural resources and claims 50 million more citizens. Yet, the U. S. has more than twice the economic output of the U.S.S.R. and three times the living standard. Why? The answer is simple. People in the Soviet Union are guaranteed everything—jobs, places to live, food, education, clothes, etc. They are literally kept from cradle to coffin. There is no incentive to do anything other than exist for the pleasure of the state. The Russian political structure disallows risk-taking because the factors of production (land, labor, capital, and management) are owned and/or controlled by the government. Consequently, individual wealth creation is impeded. Even western democratic nations that have attempted to enhance their society's "security grid" through socialist economic measures have found that economic performance suffers. France is the most recent example.

As long as 120 years ago, President Lincoln knew of the evils associated with government sponsored "blanket" security programs. He stated:

> You can't help the poor by destroying the rich.
> You can't strengthen the weak by weakening the strong.
> You can't lift the wage earner by pulling down the wage payer.
> You can't bring about prosperity by discouraging thrift.
> You can't keep out of trouble by spending more than your income.
> You can't establish social security on borrowed money.
> You can't help men by having the government tax them to do for them
>   what they should do for themselves.

Now, I am not attempting to argue against social programs *per se*. Obviously, a "security net" is a must in order to help our disadvantaged citizens who are truly needy. In addition, the lesson of the Great Depression surely exemplified the need to maintain the integrity of the country's financial structure through programs provided by the FDIC, FSLIC, and SIPC. But let's don't overdo it.

No Profits Without Risk

All of the previous sections can be related back to the individual. If you are looking for total security in an environment without risk, don't expect any dividends in the form of entrepreneurial returns. You must take a risk in order to generate revenues. The more you are willing to risk, the greater the possibility of profits. If you want all of your money protected by the FDIC, or if you are losing sleep over a $500 investment in the stock market, forget about entrepreneurship as a viable employment alternative. You may gripe and complain about your boss and the lousy pay, but you will be happier employed by somebody else as opposed to working for yourself. In other words, you do not have the proper "risk mentality" that it takes to be an entrepreneur. Sorry.

Calculating the Risk Factor

It is known from research studies that successful entrepreneurs are "moderate" risk takers. They are not the "dice rollers" that many purport them to be. The Center for Entrepreneurial Management (CEM) found that of the 2500 entrepreneurs responding to their research, 40 percent would take 3-to-1 odds at a racetrack. Fifteen percent would try 2-to-1 odds, while 23 percent would opt for a 10-to-1 shot. Twenty-two percent indicated they would go for the daily double and a chance of making a bundle.

If you are an acute risk taker and in any way have "gambling fever," don't take the entrepreneurial plunge, because you will probably lose your shirt. Even if you are a moderate risk taker, caution is still needed. You must analyze all deals in terms of risk versus reward before making a decision. Calculation is a must. Chapter XI thoroughly explains these procedures and will help you in making the right choices.

Chapter XV

Innovate for the Future

Setting Up the Innovative Environment

Many people do not distinguish between creativity and innovation, but there is a difference. Creativity is the process of creating something new or looking at things in a non-traditional way. Innovation deals with applying what has been created or identified in this process. For example, you can invent a new process to reduce manufacturing costs in your plant. This is a creative endeavor. However, innovation is not advanced unless you apply the new process to your operations. This is a fundamental problem in this country. America is viewed throughout the world as the most creative and inventive nation on the planet. On the other hand, we do not apply all of our creative output to innovative processes. Other countries procure our creative discoveries and use them in their industrial applications more effectively than we do. Countries like Japan are relieved of the research and development cost burdens, yet they can claim to be more innovative.

Mentioned below are some techniques that can be used to assist you in safely converting your new ideas into entrepreneurial innovations.

1) Scrutinize any new idea to the maximum degree possible. Don't leave any stone unturned. This provides for peace of mind.

2) Determine and record all of the negative and positive aspects of any new idea. What benefits can be expected in terms of improved marketing, lower costs, enhanced productivity, etc.? Who will receive them? Are there any risks associated with implementing the new idea? If so, what are the risks? Can a mistake be absorbed? Good managers

always visualize the worst case scenario and then make a determination as to whether they can survive that possibility. If they think not, a new idea will be forthcoming.

3) Once the idea has been analyzed for possible flaws, restructure it so that the idea is simple to understand and interpret. This will help you to clear your thinking about the new idea.

4) Review your idea with other people who may have already utilized a similar approach. Customers, competitors, consultants, accountants, and other experts could provide input. Idea weaknesses must be candidly admitted and addressed. The idea may need to be modified or even eliminated in favor of a new approach.

5) Execute the idea at the proper time. Wrong timing may cancel out the benefits of a good idea. For example, trying to execute productivity improvements using new techniques could result in a morale backlash unless employees have been properly prepared for the introduction of new methods. This orientation might take several weeks or months.

6) Evaluate the results of implementing your idea. Without proper feedback you may never know whether an idea is working until a lot of damage has been inflicted. In addition, you can monitor your batting average.

Letting It Rip

The proof of the pudding is here ladies and gentlemen. You can have all of the best ideas in the world, but if you don't convert those ideas into action nothing will be accomplished. Even if your idea turns out to be something less than a winner, at least you experimented with that particular approach and the results can be recorded for future reference. So, take the initiative and direct your creative energies into tangible innovative results. Just remember the words of Jack Paar, who said, "Life is a series of obstacles, and we ourselves are the largest obstacles." Don't fall prey to cancerous inaction. If you are willing to experiment and learn, your ability to successfully convert ideas to innovation will increase.

Keep in mind that your survival in the present and future entrepreneurial environment will depend upon your ability and willingness to apply new ideas in a changing marketplace. Many small companies are reporting that they are diversifying their product and service lines in order to stay afloat. Products and services come and go, as you have learned elsewhere in this book. You must keep abreast of your market and know when to change. Without ideas in hand ready to go, you may miss the boat. Even if the market for your products or services is growing, you still may have to engage in creative and innovative endeavors to thrive. Why is this the case? Because we find ourselves in a highly competitive economy where everybody and his brother is trying to start a business. Attraction of future customers will depend upon your success in standing apart from your competitors. In other words, doing something different, like surprising your customers with a new product or service, will help you in the game of entrepreneurship.

This brings to mind a service station owner in Virginia, who upon experiencing a drop in business decided to hire good-looking female attendants who pumped gas and washed windshields in hot pants and ultratops. What happened? Business soared, but only until other station owners reacted with their own promotional tactics. The creative station owner then counteracted by extending his hours of operation and offering a quick oil change service.

The moral to this story is clear. Creativity, innovation, and just plain guts are some essential ingredients that will ensure some degree of entrepreneurial success.

Government Help

In 1982, Congress and the President signed into existence the Small Business Innovation Development Act which authorized the Small Business Innovation Research Program, also known as SBIR. This program affords entrepreneurial firms the opportunity to promote and fund their creative innovative ideas. These ideas must meet the research/development needs of the federal government while potentially opening the door to future commercialization.

The SBIR program consists of three phases. They are:

Phase I to evaluate the scientific/technical merit and feasibility of an idea.

Phase II to expand on the results of and further pursue the development of Phase I.

Phase III for the commercialization of the results of Phase II, requiring the use of private or non-SBIR Federal funding.

The program will provide funding up to $50,000 for Phase I and up to $500,000 for Phase II if your idea has merit in terms of helping the government research and development efforts. More information about SBIR can be obtained by writing to:

Office of Innovation, Research and Technology
U. S. Small Business Administration
1441 L Street, NW, Room 500
Washington, DC 20416

Now, don't get the wrong idea here. The SBIR program is not for everybody. Only ideas of a technical nature that will help the government's research and development efforts will be considered. Also, the idea must stand a chance of commercialization in the private marketplace.

Chapter XVI

Advice for the New Breed

Ms. Entrepreneur

And who said women couldn't hack it in the business world?

Female profiteers are changing the landscape of a former male domain—entrepreneurship. The feminine side of the species has been starting new businesses at a rate that sends shivers up the spines of dedicated male chauvinist businessmen. According to President Reagan's report to Congress entitled *The State of Small Business,* women-owned businesses are the fastest growing segment of the small business population. From 1977 to 1982 the number of female nonfarm sole proprietorships increased at an annual rate of 6.9 percent compared to an overall increase of 3.7 percent for all nonfarm sole proprietorships. More specifically, from 1977 to 1982, the latest year of IRS estimates, the number of female-operated nonfarm sole proprietorships rose from 1.9 million to 2.94 million. By 1984 there were 3 million female-operated nonfarm businesses in the United States, according to U. S. Small Business Administration estimates. These figures include proprietorships, partnerships, and corporations.

Female-operated firms made strong gains in their share of total U. S. nonfarm sole proprietorships, from 22.6 percent in 1977 to 26.2 percent in 1982. For the five-year period 1977 to 1982, business receipts of female-operated nonfarm sole proprietorships increased from $25.2 to $41.7 billion, or at an average annual rate of increase of 10.6 percent. This translates into an increase in their share of total business receipts from 7.8 percent in 1977 to 9.6 percent in 1982.

Before you feminists start the victory parade, a closer look is needed to determine whether the aforementioned advances really represent good news. *The Wall Street Journal* has reported that many corporate women are joining the ranks of the self-employed because they find their career paths blocked. Since many companies are systematically reducing their employment rolls even during periods of rising revenues and profits, and with the scaling back of the affirmative action initiative, women are beginning to find the employment market tough, and meaningful job opportunities hard to locate. In addition, discrimination within corporate walls is still widespread despite the many statutory laws designed to prevent such activity. The "good old boys" are banishing women in large numbers to traditional occupational dumping groups—in particular, the corporate public relations and personnel departments. The U. S. Labor Department reported that the bulk of employed women are confined to approximately 60 occupational ranks, out of over 600 or so ranks officially recognized. Also, women are very underrepresented in the top echelons of management. Of the 100 largest companies in the country, not one can boast a lady CEO. Wage differences are also greater than ever. Women today earn 35 to 40 percent less than their male counterparts with the same level of qualifications and job responsibilities, with the gap currently increasing approximately 3 percent per year.

The aforementioned evidence suggests that these realities are "forcing" and "following" many women into the entrepreneurial camp. Despite all the good news about the increasing number of female entrepreneurs, the IRS has reported that the average net profit for women-operated firms was $1,956 compared to $6,330 for the male-operated businesses. This large disparity is of prime concern, leaving many unanswered questions. The federal government has implied that, traditionally, women possess backgrounds and academic credentials that are not conducive to the accumulation of business acumen. They further point out the fact that self-employed women are concentrated in the retail and service sectors where profits are historically lower in comparison to the manufacturing and wholesale areas where men outnumber women. But the substantial difference in net income cannot be justified that easily. Even with the recent entrepreneurial gains made by women, male entrepreneurs still outnumber self-employed females by 3 to 1. Many of these male entrepreneurs also operate in the retail and service fields.

Many small business experts contend that some female entrepreneurs are falling victim to various forms of legal discrimination because they must compromise more than males to succeed in a man's world. Many are taken lightly and treated as second-rate because a majority of them operate part-time home-based businesses. This also makes it hard to obtain credit for expansion. These intimidating conditions force some women business owners to accept lower prices for their goods or services and also to engage in unsound business arrangements where they are financially abused. To illustrate, a few years ago some unscrupulous male operators were setting up women in their own businesses and taking part ownership in the new firms. The intent was to exploit the female and take advantage of federal contract opportunities specifically directed to women-owned businesses.

Now, ladies, if after reading the previous several paragraphs you decide not to endeavor into entrepreneurship—hold on—here comes the good news.

Even with all of the difficult conditions facing the female entrepreneur, there is reason for celebration. In fact, positive conditions relating to female entrepreneuring far outweigh the negative considerations. Women today are preparing themselves for entrepreneurship. They are moving into educational and employment fields that were once male provinces.

For example, females are pushing their way into male business sanctuaries, from construction to law, with incredible speed and fortitude. Between 1972 and 1982, the number of women increased in most occupations as a percentage of total employment. Many found employment opportunities as professional and technical workers, middle-level managers, and administrators in other areas with direct entrepreneurial potential. They gained experience as computer specialists, lawyers, doctors, dentists, pharmacists, bank officials, financial managers, etc. While many women still find themselves in low-paying retail sales jobs, many are breaking ground in higher-paying marketing positions within the real estate, insurance, manufacturing, finance, and investment fields.

Within the blue-collar ranks, many more females are gaining experiences as supervisors, painters, construction and maintenance workers, telephone installers and repair technicians, butchers, welders, bus and truck drivers, gas station attendants, etc.

As women accumulate employment experience in all fields, they become more prepared to function as entrepreneurs.

Another important factor that is contributing to female entrepreneurship is the attainment of relevant education. The National Sciences Foundation recently commented on some educational gains made by women since the early 1970s.

Women accounted for more than half of the new college freshmen in 1976 and more than half of the enrollment in higher education in 1979. From 1973 to 1983 they increased their share of doctor's degrees from 18 to 34 percent. In 1983 they earned 4,470 of 17,900 science and engineering doctorates awarded and the 1983 annual gain was one of the largest over the 10-year period. Approximately 83 percent of their doctorates were in psychology (1,570 degrees), life sciences (1,360 degrees) and social sciences (790 degrees). Only 3 percent (125 degrees) were in engineering. However, the potential for women in engineering has improved greatly. Full-time enrollment of women in undergraduate engineering increased from 34,000 in 1978 to 64,600 in 1983 or by 90 percent.

The potential for business ownership and the ability to survive entrepreneurship will be greatly enhanced as women make educational gains. Education is positioning an increasing number of women for business opportunities in such fields as engineering, communications, electronics, and sciences.

Figures derived from the 1980 census show that entrepreneurial women with more than four years of college had net incomes that were 72 percent higher than the average of all female entrepreneurs in each educational grouping. In fact, the information shows that as education continually increases, so does entrepreneurial income.

Probably the greatest factor contributing to the rise of female entrepreneurship is the nation's fundamental shift from an economy based on heavy industry and agriculture to one relying on services. The service sector of the economy is expected to account for approximately 90 percent of the country's gross national product by the turn of the century. Even today, most of the new jobs created in the economy can be found in the service sector.

This shift in national emphasis has created an "entrepreneurial economy," and many women are identifying with and participating in this trend. Most service businesses are small, and most women-owned firms are in the service sector.

LADIES, DO YOU KNOW WHERE TO LOOK?

Knowing where to look for entrepreneurial opportunities is as important as being properly prepared from an educational and practical aspect.

The area of greatest growth potential for entrepreneurial opportunities over the next ten years will be in the service sector known as "miscellaneous and other services." The sector covers a large number of personal, business, amusement and recreational, medical, and professional services that by 1995 will account for 25 percent of the country's employment. Most gains will occur in business services where increases are expected for business consultants, janitorial and protective services, personnel supply, and computer and data processing services.

The service sector also includes classifications other than "miscellaneous and other services." For example, major areas of transportation, finance, real estate, utilities, communications, and the wholesale and retail trades are classified as services. The number of prospective opportunities and existing women-owned businesses are even greater under this broader definition of services.

Even though the service industries are very different, they are similar in many ways. These common characteristics lend themselves to women-owned enterprises. A lot of service industries are permeated with small-scale operations that are labor-intensive requiring little or no capital. Consequently, they are easy to enter. Some draw on skills that women have traditionally acquired in other societal roles and occupations—in human resource development, health care, education, consumer relations, and sales.

Even though most female entrepreneurs operate in areas that are traditionally women-dominated occupations, many are penetrating nontraditional fields with impressive flair. Female entrepreneurs are moving into industries such as forestry, fishing, mining, construction, manufacturing, and agricultural service. In fact, the growth rate of female-operated businesses within these industries exceeded the growth rate of the industries as a whole, according to the U. S. Small Business Administration.

Other service industries that are experiencing a growth in female-operated businesses include business, professional and health services, finance, insurance, and real estate. In addition, and more specifically, women entrepreneurs have also made substantial (more than 10 percent growth rate) inroads into the following areas:

—landscape and horticultural services
—painting, paper hanging, and decorating
—engineering and architectural services
—printing and publishing
—livestock breeding
—equipment rental and leasing
—computer and data processing services

Other businesses experiencing a moderate increase (less than 10 percent growth rate) in self-employed women include the following:

—auto repair services
—educational services
—mail order
—local and long distance trucking
—direct selling
—real estate
—recreational services
—physicians offices

Declining areas of women's business ownership include:

—motels and tourist courts
—grocery stores
—jewelry stores
—family clothing stores
—gifts, novelty, and souvenir shops

At this point it should also be pointed out that female entrepreneurs are achieving an ever-increasing share of government contracts on a federal, state, and local level. With the federal government, they recently increased their share of awards by almost 11 percent of the total value of prime contract actions over $10,000 directed to small business, while the total value of the actions decline almost 7 percent. Federal government incentives aimed at women entrepreneurs are starting to pay off for enterprising females willing to pursue the market.

Also, many female-operated firms are located in areas of high population, income, and employment. This environment is obviously conducive to the attainment of the appropriate background and experience, which can be transformed into entrepreneurial talent. In addition, markets are easier to come by in areas with large populations and incomes.

The present economy provides women with a multitude of opportunities. Recent advances in education and business experience are allowing females the ability to pursue entrepreneurship unfettered by former encumbrances. Today, women excel in many kinds of skills, knowledge, and experience needed in our service-oriented and entrepreneurial economy. Most importantly, women are providing unique perspectives in the way things are traditionally done. Sometimes this translates into an improvement in the quality and delivery of goods and services. Because females are largely new to the realm of entrepreneurship, they are not committed to particular ways of conducting business. This provides them the opportunity to be more creative and flexible in meeting the challenges of the new economy.

Minority Gains

Minorities (nonwhite) have also benefitted from the emergence of the entrepreneurial economy. Today, there are 5 percent more minority-owned businesses than in 1977. Even though this represents only a modest increase compared to female-owned firms, some unique and positive distinctions exist. For example, the net income spread between white and minority entrepreneurs averages 30.4 percent, which is significantly less than male versus female entrepreneurs, where the gap is 223.6 percent. In addition, minority entrepreneurs seem to close the income disparity more rapidly than self-employed females as educational and experience levels increase.

On the average, minority entrepreneurs tend to be younger (28 years of age) as compared to their white counterparts (43 years of age). Many small business experts contend that the lack of career opportunities force many minorities into self-employment at an earlier age. Whatever the case, many minority entrepreneurs, like women, are taking advantage of the "entrepreneurial economy." Existing self-employed minorities are concentrated in the service and retail sectors where many small firms exist and flourish. New minority enterprises will continue to penetrate these economic sectors. In addition, minority firms are exploiting opportunities in such nontraditional areas as construction, manufacturing, and wholesale.

Government initiatives, designed to promote minority entrepreneurship, have promoted a good climate for minorities seeking self-employment. Favorable contract opportunities have been translaated into a 15.8 percent increase in the amount of federal government contract money awarded to minority firms, according to the most recent information published by the Federal Procurement Data Center. This trend will most likely continue.

Also, government and private funding incentives will also serve to greatly assist minority entrepreneurs. Government directed and sponsored programs are providing thousands of minority entrepreneurs the needed liquidity to start or to buy new businesses and to expand existing enterprises. Private funding outlets such as Minority Enterprise Small Business Investment Companies (MESBICs) are specifically chartered to help prospective or existing minority entrepreneurs. They provide liquidity in the form of debt and/or equity capital. In every year since 1980, funding provided by MESBICs has increased over the previous year.

Now Is the Time

Much has been said about the difficulties faced by prospective female and minority entrepreneurs, not to mention the ones already in business. On the other hand, times couldn't be better for these groups to test the entrepreneurial waters. Government and private initiatives are providing unique opportunities. In addition, women and minorities are achieving business and relevant educational experience at a rapid rate. And let's not forget about the new "entrepreneurial economy." Today we have a unique set of circumstances that are converging at the same time. This will provide opportunities to anyone willing to take the plunge.

You can bet that before long the aforementioned events will overpower the barriers and disparities that divide the realm of entrepreneurship. This will correct the imbalances that weigh heavily against existing and prospective women and minority entrepreneurs.

So don't wait around. Now is the time to make your move.

Chapter XVII

Ushering in the New Era

The Challenges Ahead

The 1980s has been called the "decade of the entrepreneur" for good reason. More people are pursuing self-employment than at any time in our nation's history. According to the U. S. Small Business Administration the number of self-employed individuals is approaching 10 million people and increasing at a rate of 7 percent per year.

Self-expression, desire for independence, limited job opportunities, and career displacement seem to be the main reasons for the intense interest in entrepreneurship. From a demographic standpoint, members of the "baby-boom" generation appear to be responsible for this trend that is culminating in nearly one million new business starts every year.

The figures seem impressive, but the underlying realities paint a different story. President Reagan's report on *The State of Small Business* acknowledges that for every three businesses formed, two will cease to exist. Most simply go out of business for voluntary reasons. Some owners may want to retire or enter a more profitable field while others cannot hack it and move back onto the corporate career track. Ten percent cease operations for involuntary reasons and file for bankruptcy or incur large debts relative to assets and are forced to shut down.

After weighing the statistics, it would seem that about one-third of all new businesses eventually fail. Experts contend that failure is not bad because it is part of a purification process by which the economic system filters out inefficiencies. But it does leave behind debris that

177

has a profound economic and societal impact. Jobs and tax revenues are lost while some debts are never collected. In addition, those individuals suffering the trauma of defeat can inherit psychological and financial scars that may never disappear, thus inhibiting them from testing the entrepreneurial waters again.

Small business demise can be attributed to several key factors. Dun & Bradstreet reports that 92 percent of the failures are caused by lack of business acumen. Of course, this directly relates to inadequate business experience and education as well as inappropriate personality traits.

As "baby boomers," women, minorities, disenfranchised corporate executives, and large companies pursue entrepreneurial industry in an environment of moderate economic growth, competition will increase to new heights. In addition, advances in technology and innovation will shorten the life cycle of many products and services, thus changing consumer demand more frequently. This increases the risk of doing business in the marketplace. Also, as the economy becomes less predictable and more volatile, which it has over the last 10 years, business planning becomes more precarious and less reliable.

The name of the game is to be prepared for the fight of your life. Planning, flexibility, and your willingness to change will be a major factor in ensuring entrepreneurial success. To illustrate, *Wall Street Journal* reporter Steven Galante recently reported on a small company that was experiencing sales problems due to the firm's unwillingness, in prior years, to diversify into new markets. The company finally realized the need to diversify in order to survive. Its president said of its diversification, "It wasn't like a bolt out of the blue.... It was a lot of agonizing...." The president went on to say, "As technology changes, small to medium companies—especially single-product or single-market companies—are in danger of having technology eliminate their products. Companies that don't diversify in a very short time are going to trail off into the sunset." The *Journal* article went on to quote the president of another small firm having difficulty. He stated, "The fundamental problem was inflexibility.... We had single-purpose machines and single-purpose people—including single-purpose managers."

Donald L. Sexton, professor of entrepreneurship at Baylor University, summed it up by saying in the *Journal* article, "Most firms start with a single product. Those oriented toward growth immediately start looking for another one. It's that planning approach that separates the entrepreneur from the small business owner."

Protecting Your Flanks

Many entrepreneurs have found success in the marketplace because of their ability to find and exploit niches in particular markets. The famed heel maker, O'Sullivan Corporation, is an example of a company that has turned market niches into a 150-million-dollar-per-year business.

Of course, market niches are segmented portions of larger markets that traditionally go unexploited by larger firms for numerous reasons. Sometimes they are never noticed. More likely, those smaller segments are viewed as too costly to pursue and therefore will not meet profit expectations.

Not anymore, according to *The Wall Street Journal*. Faced with declining domestic and international markets, larger firms are desperately pursuing any profit opportunities that can be found or developed. Many market niches once reserved for small business activity are falling prey to profit-hungry large corporations. For example, the giant financial organization Beneficial Finance is now preparing individual tax returns, which traditionally has been a business activity dominated by self-employed tax preparers and accountants. American Express, through its Investors Diversified Services (IDS), is now providing investment planning services to individuals and families. Historically, this market has been served by CPAs, self-employed financial planners, and trust departments of local banks.

You can expect that larger companies will continue to penetrate markets that were once havens for small business activity. If they are not involved in start-up operations to exploit market niches, many will purchase existing small firms operating within niches in order to gain a foothold. Also, larger companies are acquiring existing and prospective suppliers (vendors) in an effort to achieve partial or full vertical integration (control of the entire business process from start to finish). Some entrepreneurs fall victim to the ability of their larger customers to control their destiny. Bob Nichols, the president of a two-million-dollar-per-year custom design manufacturer, complained to the researchers of this book that his largest customer buys 60 percent of the firms' output, obviously contributing to his company's financial health and stability. But, Mr. Nichols implies that on several occasions this large customer has hinted at buying his company while holding prime contracts over his head.

War on Markets

I hope that you are now convinced that enhanced entrepreneurial competition will, in fact, cause a war on all marketing fronts. So, what can you do to ensure some degree of entrepreneurial success? Well, the answer is not clear-cut, but one thing is certain. Most individuals who opt for entrepreneurship are ill-prepared for the plunge. Of course, this accounts for the large number of small business failures, even in this very robust economy. Adequate investigation coupled with appropriate education and experience are your best bets for beating the hell out of your competition.

In reference to competing with large companies, just keep in mind that technological advances and changes in lifestyles will demand more services and also encourage efficiency and creativity in the delivery of these many services. Entrepreneurs are better positioned to meet these specialized demands because they are more flexible than larger firms in mobilizing resources. This ease of movement will enable new and existing entrepreneurial firms to exploit rapid change in service distribution through the application of innovations in technology and management.

Chapter XVIII

Go for It

Let It All Hang Out

Today, we find ourselves benefitting from a unique set of economic circumstances. Falling interest rates, disinflation, decreasing oil prices, and tax reforms directed at enhancing entrepreneurial activity all seem to be converging at the same time to produce a very robust entrepreneurial environment. Times may never be better.

If you want to take the plunge, and you feel yourself ready, by all means do it now. Five years may bring a different set of economic directions that may or may not be advantageous to small business activity. But you can be sure that if you wait until the perfect time, it will never come. Remember the words of the Greek philosopher Sophocles, "Heaven never helps the man who will not act."

Never Say You're Sorry

If you have tried your hand at entrepreneurship and failed, you have nothing to feel sorry about. Even if you never attempt to take the plunge again, at some time in the future when you're sitting around the fireplace with your grandchildren on your lap, you can always tell them that you made a stab at being your own boss, unlike most people of the day who never took the risk.

This brings to mind my father. He was a failed entrepreneur who had tried his hand at wildcat coal mining, produce retailing, and beer distribution. Upon being asked about his entrepreneurial failures several weeks before his death, due to acute and prolonged heart illness, he said "I have tried what many will never attempt to do. When I leave this world don't feel sorry for me because my life has been full."

Try Again

One of several things that stood out when we were interviewing entrepreneurs for this book was their insistence that success was largely due to persistence. As mentioned earlier, some of these entrepreneurs failed more than once before hitting pay dirt. Others nursed their businesses for years before reaching what they considered success.

The theme here is simply, "Sweat buys equity." Some entrepreneurial endeavors are instant successes. There are some individuals who can smell a fad coming a year or so before it hits and position themselves to exploit it. Generally, most adventures into entrepreneurship take longer to bear fruit. If you have the patience and willingness to "stay the course," you too can enjoy the many benefits associated with self-employment. Remember the words of the famed golfer, Jack Nicklaus, who was quoted earlier. He said, "Before you learn to win, you have to learn to lose." And he should know, being the owner of over 30 business ventures.

Hero

In its quest to promote economic stability and growth, the governmental process has resorted to a number of fiscal and monetary manipulations. What has emerged is an economy of immense proportion creating jobs and wealth at a very rapid rate. Many individuals are taking credit for these successes, but one group definitely emerges as true "heroes." And these are the individuals who have been willing to absorb the risks of entrepreneurship.

Without a doubt, the political architects of the economic incentives provided in 1978 and 1981 deserve much credit, but the entrepreneurs, willing to risk everything in the marketplace, are the real sparks that have added positive dynamics to American economic progress. The resulting "entrepreneurial economy" is the envy of the world.

So, if you are a successful entrepreneur, or even one that has failed, hold yourself in high esteem, for you are the true heroes of this economy. Without you and the economic freedoms you exercise,

America would be nothing more than a second-rate nation lacking in motivation and unable to fulfill its great mission—the preservation of freedom for all to enjoy.

The Secrets

To summarize this book, it would seem that successful entrepreneurship hinges on three things. First, you must have a genuine dislike for the boss and/or your job. Second, you need to "stay the course." In other words, persistence pays dividends. Many average people have become successful entrepreneurs because of their willingness to persevere. Finally, you must have customer empathy, which is the ability to get close to your market.

If you lack any of these traits and cannot compensate for them, don't take the plunge. Save your time and money. But if you have them, by all means press on.

Appendix A

The New Product Idea

IDEAS ARE THE BEGINNING of any new product development cycle. This chapter will look at sources of ideas, the evaluation of ideas within the context of the new product development program and confront the first decision point; namely, *do you have an idea worth investigating?*

Where Do Ideas Come From?

Fortunately, this aspect of the new product process does not seem to present any real problems to the small business owner-manager or entrepreneur. Even the smallest of companies is exposed to scores of new product ideas both from internal and external sources. The problem comes when you attempt to determine if a new product idea has any merit for your company, and, as such, should be investigated in more detail.

What is a Good Idea?

A good idea is not the perfect new product idea or, more properly, should not be expected to be the perfect new product idea. Even if there were a "perfect" new product idea for your over it. "Perfect" products rarely look very attractive at first company, you probably would not recognize it if you tripped glance.

Source: U. S. Small Business Administration publication No. 39, *Decision Points in Developing New Products,* by Robert W. James.

Thus, at this point in the new product development cycle you cannot expect to be able to single out the perfect product for your company. What you can do is to determine if a new product idea has enough merit for your company to warrant further investigation. To make this determination quickly you need to know *a lot* about your own company and *a little* about the idea in question.

An Analysis Of CIRO

CIRO refers to *c*apabilities, *i*nterests, *r*esources and *o*bjectives of your company. You should have intimate knowledge of your firm's CIRO. For purposes of future decision making regarding new product ideas and opportunities, you should write out a statement of your firm's capabilities, interests, resources, and objectives. Be as specific and objective as possible. List weak points, as well as strong points. Don't try to express interest in areas where there is no interest. Goals and objectives should be as realistic as possible regarding your company's future and its resources to accomplish them.

The results of this self-appraisal can then be structured into a new product desirability profile for your company. This profile might look like the example shown below, or it might have its own unique format and style. The important thing is that the profile express what your company is all about and be a ready reference when someone comes up with a new product idea.

Company strengths

> —marketing/sales
> —cost control
> —materials research
> —excess production capacity

Company weaknesses

> —management depth
> —capital short
> —very specialized production facility—unflexible

Interests

> —becoming more active in the chemical industry
> —using our sales/marketing strengths more fully

Objectives

  —moderate growth in future
  —increased level of profits
  —protection from recession

Resources for new products

  —marketing and sales capabilities
  —materials research

Watch out for

  —high capital needs
  —unfamiliar production processes

What to Look for in a New Product Idea

Remember, at this stage of the new product development cycle, you know a lot about your own company and its CIRO, but very little, if anything, about most new product ideas that came across your desk. Does that say something about the type of decision that can be made at this point? Sounds like a gut level or seat of the pants decision, doesn't it? Almost, but not quite that bad (or good depending on your style).

The most important point upon which you can base your response to decision point number one—Do we have an idea worth investigating—is "fit." Does it fit with your CIRO and its resultant New Product Desirability Profile? Look at yourself, and look at the new product idea. Is there any fit? Try the following new produce ideas on the company profile on this and the preceding page.

- corrosion resistant coating material

- energy saving pump

- specialty bulk chemical

We all develop different images to associate with the above ideas. We really don't know very much about any of the ideas, but probably enough to determine if there is any fit with our CIRO and new product desirability profile. That's all it takes to move the new product either out of the process or into the next stage of the process.

It's Easy to Say No

The easiest decision to make with regard to a new product idea is no, no, no, no! No mess, no cost, no fuss, no further work to do. That's one way to reduce risk—don't do anything. But, of course, that also means no growth and no new products.

At this stage of the process, don't look for reasons to say no. Look for reasons to say, "Yes! There is some fit. Let's take a further look at it." Don't reject an idea that has some merit just because it isn't "perfect." On the other hand, you can't afford (more properly you don't want to afford) to look further at every idea that has any remote fit. Like many situations, you'll want to be flexible. If you have the resources available (a little time, a person to look into it, a little money), take a look at some ideas that fit. If not, be a little more choosy. The main point of this section is to guard against the natural tendency to say no all the time.

What About Lists?

New product lists are a commonplace or garden variety item in many companies. Many lists contain over a hundred new product ideas, all of which have some fit with the company. When the day comes that an idea (one single, or a couple, or several) is to be selected for further analysis, what do you do? One of the most logical methods revolves around rating the ideas against each other on a criterion or several criteria reflecting positive benefits to the company. A methodology that will essentially help you select the "best" of the list is described fully in Appendix A.

Do We Have an Idea Worth Pursuing?

The first decision that you have confronted in the new product introduction process is whether or not you even have a starting point. And, if you have a starting point, do you want to proceed to the next stage in the process? You have reached a decision point here because the next step in the process requires that we allocate some resources to learn some more about our idea. Some appropriate questions become:

- Do you want to learn more about it?

- Is there a "fit" with your CIRO?

- Do you have current resources to devote to this program?

The answer to these questions should direct you to the answer to the decision point question.

What's Next?

You have an idea. What do you do with an idea? Step back for a moment and ask the question, what is the end result of this process? Why am I going through this process? The answer can come back in many ways, but if it comes back in the form of "the development of a new business, or to launch a new product that will increase my company's revenue and sales," then the next step logically becomes to determine if the idea represents a possible product around which a profit-making business can be built; that is, a *business opportunity*. The business opportunity is the focus of the next chapter.

The Business Opportunity

PRODUCT IDEAS MUST BE TRANSLATED into business opportunities, and business opportunities must be parlayed into business opportunities *for your company* if this whole idea of new product introductions is to become a reality. This chapter will look at what constitutes a business opportunity, the development of a business opportunity model, feasibility analysis, and ultimately confront decision point number two—*do you have a valid business opportunity?*

Ideas and Opportunities

A new product idea is just that; it is an idea. It can't make you any money. It can't even give you any direction or clue as to what to do next. A business opportunity, on the other hand, can provide the basis for investment and lead to a profit-making business for your company.

A small eastern plastic molder was interested in designing and marketing proprietary products. Like most custom molders, the company was always reacting to the needs and desires of users of injection molded plastic parts and components. Since there are over 1,000 companies in the U.S. trying to capture a share of the custom molded plastic business, the major competitive factor was price and delivery. The company wanted to develop a number of products which they could market in a less competitive environment, one in which price levels would reflect the value of their unique product to the customer.

The company came up with the idea of producing a specialty designed product in the area of electronic packaging. An industrial designer was employed to come up with a propriety design, which he did. At this point, the company was faced with the question "What do we do now?" They had an idea, they even had a product. But, they had neglected to translate the idea into a business opportunity. They had no idea what *to do* with the product, or, what they *could do* with the product. No one had ever looked at the idea from the standpoint of can we build a business around this idea. The result, a significant investment in time, tooling, and product development was sitting idle as the company was forced to step back and develop the idea into a business opportunity—after the fact.

Development of the Opportunity Model

The development of a business opportunity model consists of looking at the product and the market in such a way as to be able to put your company conceptually into a business opportunity associated with the product and the market. Thus, starting with a product idea, you want to look at the product, the market, and your own company and put together a business opportunity model.

The product and the need. To form the basis for a business, a product must be associated with a need on the part of potential users of the product. No need means no business. One of the major reasons for new product failure is the fact that there was no need for the product. This tends to happen most often in technical companies where a technology is developed and perfected only to find there is no use for (much less need for) the technology.

It is possible to create a need for a product based on the introduction of the product, but this usually requires extensive advertising and/or market development programs which are outside of the scope of most small businesses. After the fact need may appear to be the rule for many consumer products that pop into the stores at Christmas time. However, the introduction of these products is probably preceded by extensive and expensive testing, research, and planning. Attempting to create a need for an already developed product is not the kind of an investment that even most large companies can tolerate and the chances of a small company succeeding in this vein is almost impossible.

In many cases your product idea will already carry a user need along with it. For example:

- A corrosion resistant coating that will protect aluminum from salt water. (This implies that there is a need to protect aluminum from salt water.)

- An air compressor that operates on $1/3$ less power than normal compressors of comparable pressure/volume specifications. (This again implies a need—for cheaper operation—associated with the product.)

- Oven racks and broiler pans that can be left in a self-cleaning oven during the cleaning cycle. (What is the user need in this instance?)

In other cases, your product idea will not be associated with a user need. With these ideas you must establish a need to go along with the product. Why? Because, it is the need statement associated with a product idea that provides the first clue of where the market for the product might exist. If there is no need that you can associate with your product idea, step back and either find a need (talk to people outside of your business—ask them what could you do with this or that) or drop your investigation of the product. Brainstorming, using a panel of creative people with different backgrounds has been one method used very successfully to "generate" uses for products or technology. A generated list should be subjected to the procedure discussed in Appendix A.

The market. The second part of your business opportunity model consists of establishing potential markets for your product. In some cases the potential markets will be quite obvious. In other cases, you will have to step back, generate (brainstorming, etc.) a list of potential markets, rank these potential markets according to their importance to your company, and settle upon several of the top markets for your product.

You now have a product idea associated with a need which has led to the identification of several potential markets. It is at this point that you can begin to see a business opportunity emerging. With our three examples presented earlier, it might look like this:

Product	Need	Market
Corrosion resistant coating	protects aluminum from salt water	• boats • buildings located near water
Air Compressor	uses ⅓ less power	• service stations • small businesses • home use
Oven racks Broiler pans	can be left in self-cleaning ovens	• home use • restaurants

Your company. The last remaining ingredient of the business opportunity model is your company. How do you fit in? Depending on your CIRO (capabilities, interests, resources, and objectives), you have more options than you probably think relative to how you could fit into the business opportunity. In most cases you will want to manufacture and sell the product and this is the assumption we will follow in this book. However, there can be very valid reasons for assuming some other position such as:

- manufacture but farm out distribution;

- distribute but farm out manufacturing;

- develop concept and license to others;

- develop concept and sell completely;

You now have a business concept. It might read like this:

Waldorf Company will finalize development of a new corrosion resistant coating designed to protect aluminum from salt water. The product will be manufactured in our own plant and marketed to building products distributors and boat builders.

Feasibility Analysis

The importance of a business opportunity model lies partially in directing your thinking in the direction of business, and away from a product, and partially in providing you with a business model to check out, refine, revise, and improve by performing a feasibility analysis.

Most business opportunity models do not survive the feasibility analysis without being revised in a major way. You should expect this to happen and guard against being resistant to any changes. In fact, a fairly high percentage of business opportunity models will be proven invalid during this analysis, and dropped entirely. It is a lot cheaper to find out at this stage that a new product is not worth your company's investment than to discover the bad news after major resources are committed.

A feasibility analysis is a process designed to check the validity of your business opportunity model and to provide you with enough information to confront decision point number two—*Do we have a valid business opportunity?* A feasibility analysis consists of the following parts:

- develop initial criteria
- develop a product profile
- determine information needs
- gather information
- analyze results

Develop criteria. In order to be able to accurately assess the potential worth of your business opportunity, you should attempt to set up some business guidelines which reflect your views of what your company needs or desires from your new product in the way of:

- sales volume (minimum/maximum)
- time required to obtain market penetration
- profit potential
- investment level
- number of customers
- geographical limitations
- other factors important to *you*

Develop a product profile. In all cases where your business opportunity consists of marketing a proprietary product, you will need some kind of a product description, profile, or data sheet to describe your planned offering to potential customers. The basic purpose of the product profile is to provide your potential customer with enough information to allow him to provide some feedback to you regarding your product. If your product is a service or a well-known product, the needs for a product profile still remain, but should be oriented towards what service you are offering or what benefits the potential customer might derive in doing business with you (in terms of an established product).

You should strive to communicate as much information as can be quickly presented and understood by a potential customer. Keep it as simple as possible. You are not trying to sell the product or service—you are trying to get feedback on interest and need. You might consider including the following types of information [1] in your product profile:

- description—functional and aesthetic

- specifications—technical details or planned specifications

- benefits to the user

- advantages over competitive products

- disadvantages compared to competitive products

- projected price

- other appropriate information

- models or samples are helpful

A sample of a product profile that might be used during a feasibility analysis of a new product is presented in Appendix B.

Determine information needs. In performing a feasibility analysis of your business opportunity, you should strive to learn as much as possible about the market for your product, the potential customers, competition, and your product itself, as perceived by the potential customer. To this end, you want to prepare a list of information needs which can be translated into questions that you will want to discuss with potential customers and other sources of information. You might want to include the following:

---

[1] Not all of this information may be known at the time of the feasibility study. Indeed, some of the above may be determined during the feasibility study. If unknown, ask.

- what is currently used—why
- what advantages does your product have
- what disadvantages does your product have
- what is the need for a new supplier
- who specifies, designs and buys products like yours
- how are these kinds of products usually sold
- price levels
- competition
- volume of usage/order frequency
- what kind of company (industry, size, etc.) needs your product
- other factors that may determine purchase such as guarantees, delivery, terms, discounts

Gather information. There are many ways to gather the information necessary to answer the kinds of questions presented above. This would include secondary sources such as trade magazines, product literature from competitors, government statistics, mail surveys using questionnaires, telephone interviewing, and personal field interviewing of potential customers. Each of these methods will produce information at a relative cost and in relative depth and accuracy. Table I attempts to compare the methods.

Selection of the sample to be contacted should include as wide a range of potential customers as possible given your budget and time. Large as well as small companies, distributors, competitors (often the source of excellent information), and existing users as well as non-users should be included in your sample. The purpose in expanding the sample to include various kinds of contacts is to make your survey as reliable as possible.

How much contact should you make? Enough to satisfy yourself that the answers you are getting back are a true reflection of the true state of the market. It is hard to predict how much will be enough, but you will be able to tell when you have enough by the fact that answers you are receiving become repetitive or form a pattern or trend.

Oftentimes it is a good idea to have someone outside your

company perform the feasibility analysis to eliminate your own bias as well as to get the job done more efficiently and quickly. There are many well-qualified professional service firms equipped to do this kind of work for your company. How do you find one? Ask your friends in other businesses, use directories or the yellow pages. Talk to several firms and pick the one that feels the best to you. Be careful about experts who profess to know all there is to know about products like yours. If your product is really new—no one is an expert.

Analyze results. The results of your information gathering should be analyzed in line with the initial criteria you developed. If the results point out deficiencies in the business potential associated with your opportunity, determine if there is something that can be done to eliminate the problem, increase the potential, or modify the criteria.

Is This a Valid Business Opportunity?

This decision point may be the most important one you will encounter during the new product development cycle. Here is where you will eliminate the large majority of the product ideas you consider. In a sense, this decision point gets your new product idea out of committee and into the pipeline.

The feasibility analysis has required that you learn a lot about your new product as a potential business opportunity for your company. You must consider the results of the feasibility analysis in light of the business opportunity model and your own success factors. Then you must make a very practical judgment of whether there is really a business opportunity associated with your new product. You have as much information as you'll ever have, so don't be afraid to make a decision.

What's Next?

The financial analysis of business opportunities is the next topic. This analysis is designed to provide you with more information on which to base future business decisions regarding your new product.

TABLE I. *Comparison of information gathering techniques*

Method	Cost	Kinds of information that can be developed	Problems
Secondary source	Low (time only)	Macro statistics Trends Competition	Tends to be historical—does not give you direct feedback on your product. Will not find out whether your product will succeed.
Mail	Medium ($5 per source)	Potential interest Current usage Competition	Low response rate. Not direct feedback on your product. May be inaccurate. No way to interact and probe.
Telephone interviews	Medium ($10 per source)	All information	Difficult to describe product via phone in many cases. Mail plus phone follow-up may overcome this problem. Interaction possible.
Personal field interviews	High ($50 or more per source)	All information	Best way to get information. Most expensive. Can interact and probe.

Venture Analysis

N O MATTER HOW UNIQUE your new product is, or how large the potential market appears to be, if you cannot make a profit producing and selling the product, there is no reason to go into the business. In this section we will confront the decision point question—*is your new product profitable?* A simplified financial analysis technique will be used which will be termed venture analysis.

The Process

Venture analysis can offer your company a relatively inexpensive financial preview of the projected profitability of your new product. Venture analysis cannot make your new product a winner, but it might tell you if there is any hope of making a winner out of your new product. Venture analysis can help to give you an objective view of the future at a point in time when it is not too late or too expensive to make some changes or even drop the product. In other words, venture analysis can be a useful tool to help keep you from introducing a new product that does not have a chance of being profitable no matter how successful it may be in the marketplace.

Venture analysis is not a replacement for a full blown financial analysis that normally accompanies a new product business plan as it vies for investors' financial support. On the other hand, a venture analysis does not require a CPA to prepare it, or to understand it. In short, venture analysis is short on nitty gritty detail and long on insight which is what you need to supply you with feedback when you need it the most.

In its simplest form (and part of the beauty is its simplicity), a venture analysis for a potential new product would necessarily include the following:

1. A schedule of the major items involved in the creation of "the business" which will chronologically examine elements such as capital investment, production, inventory build-up, sales, and manpower utilization for the time period up to and through start-up and continuing until projected stability is reached.

2. A cash flow analysis and pro forma income statement for the time period covered above.

3. A pro forma balance sheet presenting a year-end summary of the financial position of the venture during the covered time period.

4. Several supporting schedules providing standard product costs, capital equipment and facilities costs, and manpower costs and utilization.

An Example

It is important to realize that this is a financial preview to give your company a projected view of the future. As such, it uses realistic estimates for sales volume, product costs, fixed costs, and overhead. Don't get hung up on details—use your best estimates for the following:

1. Investment in plant and equipment including engineering and installation.

2. Other pre-startup costs should also be capitalized and included in the capital investment required by the business.

3. Standard product cost (variable and fixed should be separated).

4. Selling price, taxes, interest expenses on debt capital if required.

5. Depreciation on plant and equipment.

You will note that we are using the contribution margin (difference between sales revenue and *variable* cost of goods sold) approach to the income and cash flow statement. This is a straightforward and useful way of looking at the financial state of a new venture. In this approach, all truly fixed costs are expenses during the time period in which they were spent. No fixed costs are allocated to product costs for inventory purposes. Thus the contribution margin becomes the amount of money available to pay fixed costs and profit, and the relationships between cost, volume, and profit for the business can be quickly seen. The following example will illustrate this method.

TABLE II. *Estimated values for venture analysis*

Capital investment: $40,000 required.
Production: During first quarter—1,000 units
                    2nd quarter on   —2,000 units
Sales: During first quarter—sell 100 units, inventory 900
          2nd quarter—sell 1500 units, inventory 500
          3rd quarter—sell 2000 units.
Selling price: $10 per unit
Product costs:
          Variable $5 per unit
          Fixed $4,000 per quarter
          Depreciation $1,000 per quarter
Tax: Assume 50 percent total

The above is a best guess based on as much information as is available at the time of the venture analysis. As more information is available, the analysis would be performed again. With the above information, the cash flow and income statement on page 24 could be prepared.

Analysis

The information contained in the above income and cash flow statement is enough to completely analyze the projected financial performance of your new product. The following kinds of analysis can be made:

Breakeven point. Use a graphical method as shown in figure 2 using variable costs, selling price, and fixed costs.

TABLE III. *Pro forma income and cash flow statement*

Ajax Mfg. Co.
Venture #42

	Pre Start-up	QUARTER 1	2	3	4
Inventory (beginning)	0	0	900	1400	1400
Production	0	1000	2000	2000	2000
Sales	0	100	1500	2000	2000
Inventory (ending)	0	900	1400	1400	1400
Investment	40000				
Revenue (from sales)		1000	15000	20000	20000
Less variable cost of goods sold		500	7500	10000	10000
Contribution margin		500	7500	10000	10000
Less fixed costs [1]		9500	7500	5000	5000
Gross operating margin (loss)		(9000)	0	5000	5000
Tax (50%) (loss carry fwd.)		0	0	0	500
Net income (loss)		(9000)	(0)	5000	4500
Depreciation [2]		1000	1000	1000	1000
Cash flow	(40000)	(8000)	1000	6000	5500
Cumulative cash flow	(40000)	(48000)	(47000)	(41000)	(35500)

[1] Include $4000 per quarter for fixed costs, $1000 per quarter for depreciation, and any increase in inventory at $5 variable cost per unit.

[2] Depreciation is a non-cash expense. Thus, to determine cash flow depreciation is added to net income.

Graphical Analysis of Breakeven Point

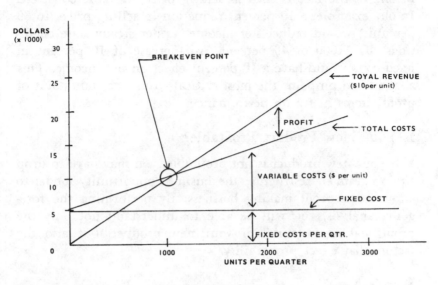

Figure 2.

In this example, the breakeven point occurs at 1000 units per quarter. You can also see from the above graph what effect an increase or decrease in selling price or fixed costs or variable costs will have on the breakeven point.

Working capital needs. The amount of money needed to finance the business must include not only the investment in plant and equipment but also money to finance early losses until cash flow turns positive. In our example, cash flow turns positive during the second quarter. A total of $48,000 is thus required to finance this business. (For longer time periods—discounting is required to reflect the time value of money).

Return on investment. The investment in our example totals $48,000. During the first year net income was $500 for a rate of return of slightly more than 1 percent. Under steady state conditions, the business would show a net income of $2500 per quarter or $10,000 per year. This would yield a simple after tax return on investment of a little more than 20 percent. Discounted rate of return analysis should be used for longer time periods.

Sensitivity analysis. A very useful analysis can be made of a venture by analyzing the effect on net profit caused by a change in one of the factors such as selling price, variable costs, etc. In our example, a 10 percent reduction in selling price (to $9 per unit) would reduce net income (under steady state conditions) by $1000 or 40 percent. An increase of 10 percent in fixed costs would have a 10 percent effect on net income. This analysis can pinpoint the most critical (from the standpoint of profit) items in future performance.

Is Your New Product Profitable?

If your new product is not profitable, you may have to drop the program or restructure the business opportunity model to allow for a profit making business. By performing the foregoing analysis, you will be able to understand not only the profit making potential of your new product, but also the factors that effect profitability.

What's Next?

The remainder of this book will be devoted to developing the new product and its associated business venture into an operating entity. Product design and development, marketing strategy, production, planning, and building a business will be covered in that order.

Product Design and Development

T HE DESIGN AND DEVELOPMENT of your product is the tie
between your product idea in its present form and the
marketplace your business thrust is aimed at. The design and
development phase has as its goal to develop a commercially
acceptable product that can be sold and manufactured at a
profit by your company. Associated with the design and development phase of the new product introduction process are at
least four decision point subquestions:

- Can a commercial product be developed?
- Will the design sell?
- Can it be produced?
- Can we afford the cost of development?

Can a commercial product be developed? Not every product
idea can be developed into a commercial reality. Technology
may be the stumbling block, or money, or getting the product
to function in service as it does in the laboratory. It is important to periodically assess the chances of commercial success
in your product development effort.

Will the design sell? The goal of product design and development is to produce a product that can be sold in a competitive marketplace. Keep asking this question and continue to get feedback as your design finalizes. Design to factors and features that are important to the potential user, not to features that are only important to you. Don't forget to look for design features that can give you a competitive edge.

Can it be produced? Not everything can be produced in commercial quantities. Sometimes pilot plants cannot be scaled up, capital costs become too high to produce the product, production costs exceed value of product to user, or other problems may render your idea interesting, but impossible to exploit.

Can you afford the cost of development? New product develment programs have a way of being so exciting to those involved that everyone loses sight of how much the program is costing versus the progress that is being made or planned. Don't lose sight of the bottom line.

Product Research and Development

The need for research and development activities during the new product introduction process depends on the degree to which your product idea is a commercial product. If your new product is in the form of some patented or proprietary technology which you plan to apply to a specific commercial venture, the amount of R & D involved in taking your product from concept to commercial success will probably be significant. In other cases (primarily low technology areas), the necessary involvement of R & D may be quite minimal. Whatever the level of involvement, it is important to keep the reason for R & D's existence well in mind: *to make commercial products out of ideas and technology.*

The following aspects of product research and development are worth discussing:

- direction

- proprietary position

- patents and protection

- costs

Direction. The direction taken in developing your new product idea into a commercial reality should be guided by a very practical, goal-oriented objective. That is, you want to develop a product that will satisfy the needs of the potential user of the product. Your business opportunity model and your feasibility analysis should provide you with a clear idea of where you're headed, or should be headed, in the development process.

Don't let the process turn around such that you are developing products or technology which you will then "check out" to see if there is any market or need for. Also, don't try to solve impossible development problems or try to tackle development tasks way beyond the scope or capability of your company's resources. Recognize when you can efficiently do development work in-house and when it would be more cost effective to go to a contract research and development firm to accomplish specific tasks or subtasks.

Proprietary position. One of the reasons that companies engage in product research and development activities is to develop a competitive edge in design over their competition in the marketplace. This should be one of the objectives of your product development program: namely, to develop a product that is unique in some way such that your product is set apart from the competition.

Your feasibility analysis should have identified a number of design factors that are important to potential users of your product. Direct your product development efforts in the direction of consumer wants and in the direction of developing a competitive edge. Unless your development effort is geared to making your product competitive, you might as well copy existing products, put your name on them, and save the development money for some other aspect of your business.

There are many products for which there is no unique design available. In this case, your uniqueness is going to have to come from another direction such as packaging, service, marketing or sales programs, guarantees, or even price. Thus, to be economically sound, a product must have a unique feature. "Me too" is not enough.

Patents and protection. Patents can offer a degree of protection for your new product. They make it more difficult for competition to enter the market with a copy of your product.

However, in many cases a patent may do nothing other than feed the ego of the developer and the bank account of your attorney. Do not jump into patenting product design features or process innovations without considering the implications of a patent; namely, it is a published discussion of how you designed your product. There may be other ways to protect yourself. One company deliberately obtained a process patent to lead their competition away from the way they were actually producing their product. The actual process design was kept a well-guarded secret.

Costs. The costs of research and development can become a real burden on the financial position of your company. Many people advocate unbudgeted research and development projects to allow the creative talents of the researchers to shine. If you want to develop your new product idea into a commercial product for a cost that will allow you to make a profit, make your research budgets as tight and as goal oriented as any budget area in your company.

Demand continually updated information on research and developement cost estimates, as well as target dates, design criteria, technical problems and planned solutions, and chances of success. This material needs to be reviewed often. Questions of costs and questions of how much and for how long the program should be backed must be asked often.

Design

The design of a new product will have a lot to do with your success or lack of success in the marketplace. The design of your new product should be determined by an orientation to the marketplace (a design that will sell) and an orientation to production and cost control (a design that can be efficiently produced).

Marketplace orientation. The marketplace for your new product can provide you with all the design criteria you need to completely design your product. The biggest problem will not be to determine what the market wants, but to put *all* the features together into a package that can be produced, sold, serviced, inventoried—all at profit. Your product cannot be all things to all people, but its design can be based on maximizing its appeal to the potential purchaser while still being consistent with practical design constraints.

Production orientation. Some thought should be given to how you are going to produce your product at a cost that will allow for a competitive price and a reasonable level of profit. Designing for efficient production involves considering a lot of factors including existing production facilities, availability of capital, production volume, product life, competition, etc. The final design criteria selected should reflect a combination of factors, including the marketplace, production costs, and efficiency.

Design Criteria

The following criteria should be considered during the design phase of the new product introduction process. This is not intended to be an exhaustive list but to challenge your thinking relative to good design, and to point out that design criteria should be based on accomplishing your business objectives and implementing strategy.

Cost/volume/profit relationships. The price of your product will be a major factor in determining the volume of product you sell. This, in turn, makes the cost of producing that volume critical to the profitability of your business. Based on some idea of the price/volume relationship for your product, a production cost criterion can be developed.

Competition/proprietary appeal. The design of your product should offer it some competitive strengths in the marketplace. The needs of users plus the products now on the market should help you develop criteria leading to a strong competitive position for your product. More about product differentiation in the chapter on marketing strategy.

Product line possibilities. The design of your product may be influenced by the possibility of, or the necessity of, offering a product line consisting of a number of different sizes or types of product, a modular design incorporating a number of different products, or a series of products aimed at the same market. Design compatibility between all of a company's products should be considered as a way to pass on company good will.

User specifications. The function or use to which your product will be put may impose various design criteria relating to user specifications for installation, safety, service, codes, reliability, and performance. It is necessary that you develop detailed technical and design criteria *in conjunction with* your potential customers so that you will not be faced with expensive, after the fact, design changes.

Options and accessories. In order to successfully sell your product you may need to offer various options and accessories or provision for same. Your design should take this into account.

Quality/service/warrantee. All of these items may be required to be competitive in the marketplace, and if your product cannot be sold without an adequate guarantee, you had better know about it before your design is finalized.

Packaging/shipment/storage. These factors may enter into the design of your product.

Manufacturing. Process selection, make-buy decisions, materials of construction, and other important manufacturing variables all could be important outcomes of the product design and need to be considered.

Design and Development in Perspective

The design and development of your new product is concerned with making a commercial reality out of a product idea. The product design and development process should be geared to accomplishing the objective of making the product more saleable in the marketplace or easier to produce in the factory. As such, your design should be guided by the marketplace, your competition, your customers, cost-volume-profit relationships, and the answers to the four decision point questions.

1. *Can a commercial product be developed—at an acceptable cost?* If not, either modify the product such that it can be developed, increase financial support, or drop the program.

2. *Will the design sell?* Your design should be based on establishing a strong competitive position in the marketplace. Keep your design moving in the right direction by continuing to ask this question and making changes, if necessary.

3. *Can it be produced?* If it can't, change your design or modify your production capabilities, or drop the project.

4. *Can we afford the cost of development?* Continue to ask this question along with questioning the overall profitability of

the new product. Remember, you are in business to make a profit and a return on the investment.

What's Next?

The next topic will involve developing a market strategy for your new product. The basic question to be asked is, "Can the product be sold?"

Marketing Strategy

THE BASIC OBJECTIVE in developing a marketing strategy is to match your capabilities and the characteristics of your product to the characteristics of the marketplace your product will compete in. The task in developing a marketing strategy is to understand the inner workings of the marketplace and to position your product *and* your company in a way that will accomplish your objectives.

Objectives

Objectives are important to the development of marketing strategy because they define where you want to end up. Your marketing strategy, like a map, will help you get there. Marketing objectives are a reflection of overall company objectives, and should be formulated such that there are specific goals and objectives to aim at and to measure performance against.

Your new products must fit into the overall scheme of things and, thus, there should be definite goals and objectives for each new product. In order to be effective, these goals and objectives should reflect the fact that the product is new and that there is a need for flexibility. Goals should be specific enough that performance can be measured as well as realistic enough that success is possible. The time frame for any goal should be short enough to motivate action, and in no case longer than one year. In addition, goals should not be concerned with how the objectives are accomplished, just what level of accomplishment is desired. Marketing goals and objectives might be appropriate for your new product in the following categories:

- sales volume
- number of stocking distributors
- profit on sales
- market share
- volume of reorders
- new customers
- specific customers

Market Research

Market research and development is thought of by many as a more important form of research than product research and development. Just as a developed product is the output of product research and development, a developed marketing strategy is the output of market research and development.

If you are really serious about your new product introduction, and, if you really want to succeed in the marketplace, don't shortchange market research and development. A brief review of the market research function as it applies to the development of marketing strategy is outlined below.

Kinds of information. Basically, what you need to know about a market to develop a marketing strategy is:

1. Who are the potential customers for this product?
2. Will they buy this product?
3. Why do they buy products like this?

In addition, you can learn a lot about the mechanics of the marketplace for your new product that will provide you with background information that can prove very useful in the development and implementation of a marketing strategy.

Sources of information. Sources of market research or marketplace-based information include market research surveys of all types (review feasibility analysis in Chapter 3), test market programs, trade publications, industry associations, knowledgeable individuals, and other primary and secondary sources of information. Probably the most straightforward method for you to develop the answers to the three questions above would be to go out (either yourself or hire a consultant) and ask a sample of potential users and persons in the distribution channels. Ask enough such that you can answer the three questions and feel confident that your answers reflect the true state of the marketplace.

When should you do market research? Market research will yield valuable information any time you are developing a marketing strategy for a new product, planning to enter a new market area with existing products, or looking for or at new products or new market opportunities. Appendix C contains several examples relating to the need to look at the marketplace before selecting a marketing or sales strategy.

Understanding the Marketplace

A complete understanding of the marketplace as it relates to your specific new product and its associated business opportunity will include an understanding of the following items.

Market definition. Where will your product be directed? List the industries or segments of the public that represent the best potential for your product and describe the channels of distribution you will use to deliver your product to them.

Market segments. Are the broad market areas defined above homogeneous or can they be further subdivided into smaller segments which could profit by their own marketing strategy or sales coverage? How large or important are the various segments? Should some be targeted or dropped because they are *too* small or *too* different? For example, you may find that 95 percent of the potential market for your new product lies in the chemical industry, while 5 percent lies with the home hobbiest or handyman.

Size of market. While this information is somewhat useful, it is not useful enough to spend a lot of time and expense attempting to come up with an accurate prediction of the total market for X in 1985. More important is the order of magnitude of the total market for X in 1985. Would it make any difference to you if the total market for X was $50 million or $40 million or $60 million? Probably not. It would make a difference in your thinking and strategy if the market were $5 million or $500 million. Also, you are more concerned about the market for *your* "washing machine" than you are about the market for washing machines in general.

Trends. Is the market for your new product growing? Declining? Stagnant? Your marketing strategy will be dependent on your understanding of future trends that are likely to occur in the marketplace. A declining or stagnant market need not mean the end to your new product dreams. It may tell you that to be successful you will have to create a new market for your product, or that your strategy will include a quick in and out sales campaign followed by getting out of the business—with a profit.

Mechanics. The so-called mechanics of the marketplace refers to the inner workings of the relationship between buyer, seller, and manufacturer. Your understanding of "who is doing what to whom" is critical to the development of a marketing strategy that will work. The following might give you an idea of what kinds of information you are looking for in this area.

- who specifies what brand is purchased
- who buys
- who designs
- how are specifications developed
- what factors are considered most important
- lead time
- order quantities
- bid requirements
- etc.

Competition. Who else is producing and/or selling your kind of product? How successful are they? Answers to these questions will help you develop a good, sound, and field-tested marketing strategy. Especially look at the strongest supplier in the market. He must be doing something right to be where he is.

Understanding Your Product

In order to formulate a marketing strategy for your new product you should have a good understanding of your own product as it relates to the marketplace, including the user view of your product, the potential for your product, and the real need for your product.

User view. What does the potential user of your product think about your product and the other competing products? Your marketing strategy will want to overcome problems the user may have with your product and capitalize on the advantages of your product. Thus, you should solicit user opinions on your product and what advantages or disadvantages it may have relative to competition. The big selling point you thought your product possessed may not be very important to potential customers, and other characteristics of your product may be seen as definite advantages by the potential user. Users may also suggest basic improvements which would make your product more appealing. Listen to the marketplace. It can tell you a lot about your own product. It is not what you think about your product, or how "good" or technically superior your product may be, but what the buyer thinks that determines what product is purchased. Your product development and technical people will tell you how great your new product is compared to competition. Don't believe them. Ask the user, he's the one you have to sell.

Potential for your product. No matter how big the market for washing machines was last year, and no matter how much growth is expected next year, the key to your success is how many of your washing machines will sell next year. Market research that tells you more than you ever wanted to know about what happened to washing machine sales over the past 20 years and the trend for the next 10 years may be interesting, but useless when it comes to pragmatic decision making and strategy development. In order to know the potential for your product, you need to know if anyone will buy it, why they will buy it, and how much they would pay for it. The key point here is that you should not rely on industry-wide statistics to determine the potential for your product. You need direct feedback from real users and from the sales chain. For example, even if the user wants the product, a distributor or dealer may not handle it because of discounts, conflicts with larger product lines, financing, and so on.

Just as in the feasibility analysis, take your product (the real thing or a data sheet describing your product) into the marketplace; don't try to sell it to anyone; describe it and ask "what do you think about it?" Probe why the person likes it or does not like it. Be careful to make your question open ended; do not answer your own question by selling the product. Let the respondent answer in the way he really feels. Accurate information can be obtained, but you have to allow it to come out during the interview. Your position as interviewer should be as unbiased as possible and even slightly negative towards your own product if you must show some bias.

The market potential for your product can be estimated by taking the total market estimate and estimating market penetration or market share for your product based on your experience out in the field plus other information concerning planned level of sales activity, geographical limitations, ability to produce and deliver, and others. You should be able to come up with a figure that represents a pretty accurate order-of-magnitude estimate of what you might expect in the way of sales volume for your new product.

Need for your product. In talking to potential users about your product, you will very quickly find out one very important aspect of the market for your product: how much do people need your product, how much do people need another supplier of that kind of product, or how interested or excited are potential customers about your product or your company. This point of information can be very important to the development of a marketing strategy because you may have to follow a strategy that will somehow create interest in order to successfully reach the marketplace with a new product.

However, if you do not feel comfortable about your estimates of total market and your company's penetration, you may survey the distribution channels and ask them how many they think they could sell. Another way is to show your product in a trade show—but only if you are prepared to take immediate advantage of the results.

Strategy Development

The question you are attempting to answer through the development of a marketing strategy is, "Can this product be sold?" The answer that you will hopefully give is, "'Yes, if we approach it using this strategy." Your marketing strategy will consist of a number of elements including:

- Business definition
- Customer definition
- Market segmentation
- Product differentiation
- Sales and distribution
- Promotional activities
- Pricing policies
- Entry strategy

Business definition. What kind of business are you in? Do you perform a service for your customers or do you simply sell a product?

In some cases, it may not be immediately clear exactly how you want to approach your new product/market. Some companies that sell custom products such as molded plastic parts and components, castings, and customized business forms are really service businesses, while some companies supplying services are really in a product business such as photographers.

A definition of what kind of business you are in should include a statement of what you are selling and what the customer is buying. What need is being satisfied and what process of satisfaction is being followed. Is your product completely satisfying the need, or are other product or service inputs required? Is your product the leading or lagging product in the need satisfaction process?

Customer definition. Just as with what kind of business you are in, there may be some uncertainty regarding who are your real customers. In many cases you may not be selling your product to the person with the need you are satisfying. If your product is being sold to the person or company with the need, your marketing strategy will be different than if your customer uses your product as a component part or a raw material for his product.

In some instances one element of your marketing strategy may be to determine who your customer should be. One suggestion is to select as the customer that person your new product does the most good for. For example, if your new product will help save a foundry manager over 40 percent of his electric bill, sell the product direct to the foundries rather than to the hot metal storage facility producers, even though your product has to be installed on their equipment.

A definition of your customer should include why you are selling to *him* and why he is buying from you. What's in it for each of you? Who else could you sell it to, and why have you decided not to?

Market segmentation. Your marketing strategy should recognize the various segments of the market for your new product. All market segments should be analyzed from the standpoint of what is different about:

- the way the customers view your product,
- the way the customers buy products like yours,
- how much your product is worth to them, and
- what other options they have.

Your marketing strategy should take the above into account and examine the potential represented by each segment. This will lead you to a strategy consistent with the realities of the marketplace. One advantage of segmenting the market for your product is that you can home in on a specific market segment where your product has its greatest potential/appeal. Instead of marketing a product in one way to everyone you are recognizing that some segments are not only different, but better than others for your product.

Market segmentation will require you to adjust your product and marketing strategy to recognize the separate and distinct markets for your new product. This can be of great help in penetrating a market which would be too broad and undefined without segmentation.

Product differentiation. Any discussion of market segmentation should be followed by a discussion of product differentiation. You must recognize that your new product cannot be all things to all people. It might be better strategy to gear your product or your marketing strategy and product design to one segment of the total market. Highest quality, lowest price, or high style are examples of this.

To see the relationship between product differentiation and market segmentation, think of the total potential market for your new product as the whole pie. Market segments are represented by wedges as in the familiar pie chart. Market segmentation seeks to secure market penetration in one or more wedge-shaped pieces while product differentiation seeks to secure a layer of market share over the entire market.

Product differentiation is best accomplished by setting your product apart from the other products in your industry. This is most often accomplished through design, color, packaging and the promotion and advertising of these differences to the marketplace. A good marketing strategy may use both product differentiation *and* market segmentation to advantage.

It is important to remember that your marketing strategy can and should change to meet the current condition of the market for your product. The ability of your company to adjust to the changing condition of the marketplace will be greatly enhanced by an up-to-date knowledge of the marketplace. You must continually monitor the marketplace using the techniques of market research.

Sales and distribution. Your market research should have identified what kind of sales and distribution system is required by the marketplace. If a product obviously requires a direct selling technique by a technically knowledgeable individual, you will want to establish a sales mechanism that you can provide that kind of direct coverage. There are a number of alternatives for your company to select from including direct salesmen, manufacturers representatives and distributors.

Direct salesmen are employed by you to sell *your* product. As such, you can direct their efforts towards or away from specific market segments, you can provide them with very specific training, and, in short, you can control and guide what they sell and where they direct their sales effort. For this control, you will have to provide support in the form of a salary or a draw against future sales commissions. Generally, if a salesman can support himself in a given territory, use this method. That is, will the sales volume be sufficient so that the percentage paid to a direct salesman would cover his salary, expenses, and so on?

Manufacturers reps usually represent a number of manufacturers and actively promote a line of products, all of which are promoted and sold to the same general type of customers. Reps are paid a commission on their sales volume. No sales, no commission. You can suggest where the rep might direct his selling effort, but unless he makes sales in those areas, he will quickly move towards areas where he *can* sell your product.

Distributors generally carry a number of lines of products and will stock an inventory of these products. They promote sales through catalogues and salesmen and direct their sales efforts in a geographic area.

Several important characteristics of the sales function for your new product include how much time and effort is needed to sell your product, dollar value of a sale, service required, time allowed for delivery, and number of customers in a geographic area. The three traditional sales methods are discussed relative to these characteristics in the table on p. 44. The characteristics of the marketplace and/or your product are listed and a + or − rating is given each sales method to indicate relative performance on that factor. For example, if a lot of time is required to sell your product, direct sales is the method to consider. Your choice of method should be made by taking into account the characteristics listed in the table plus characteristics of your own product/market.

Promotional activities. Promotional activities include all forms of communications between your product and the potential customer for your product. This includes advertising, catalogue sheets, press releases, and technical articles. Again, your market research information should provide you with guidance on how to promote your new product. Promotional material should be designed to promote those aspects of your product and your company that are important to the potential user of your product. The features and benefits of your product and your company that are important to the user will probably change over time, and, as such, your promotional programs should change and adjust to changing conditions in the marketplace.

You should never promote your company or your products just for the sake of promoting. Every piece of promotional material and every advertisement of your products should have a *specific* objective and a specific message and design to accomplish that objective. If you do not have an objective, do not advertise. You should never fall into the trap of allocating X percent of sales for advertising and then look for ways to spend that much money through some advertising agency. However, using a percentage of sales may be a valuable *guide* in planning your advertising budget.

TABLE IV. *Relative performance of various sales methods as a function of product/market characteristics.*

Characteristics	Direct	Reps	Dist.
A lot of time required to sell the product	+	–	–
Low cost of sales desired			
high volume period	+	–	0
low volume period	–	+	0
Ability to direct sales efforts	+	–	–
Ability to provide "service" to the end user in form of delivery and other assistance	0	–	+
Low $ value per sale	–	–	+
Feedback from field on customers and your products	+	0	–
A lot of market development required on a new product	+	–	–

A selection of media for your advertising should be based on where and how you can reach the people that are affected by advertising of your product. It may turn out that the only form of promotion that makes any difference at all is a personal sales call backed up by good quality technical literature. Space advertising in this case would be a waste of money.

In summary, the promotional aspects of your new product marketing strategy should be guided by the following:

1. Promote the benefits and features that are important to potential users of your product.

2. Promotional programs should have very specific objectives and should be designed to accomplish those objectives. If you don't have an objective—don't advertise.

3. Promotional needs will change as the condition of the marketplace changes.

4. Selection of media should be based on reaching those persons that can be affected by your advertising and that have some influence in the purchase decision.

5. Be aware of the different market segments for your product and the opportunity to promote your product in different ways to different segments of the market.

Pricing. The pricing policy used for your new product should be based on an understanding of the cost-volume-profit relationship. The price you place on your product needs to be based on competition in the marketplace and on generating a profit for your company.

The analysis of profitability that was presented in Chapter 4 is valid in this case as a pricing tool. Develop the cost-volume-profit relationship for your new product starting with the best cost analysis you can make. Once you understand the relationship between cost, volume of sales, and profit, you can analyze the marketplace, including competitive price levels and market share possibilities. Also, you can include your own requirements, such as required return on invested capital, etc.

The marketing strategy that you develop for your new product will have something to say about the pricing strategy you decide to use. For example, two of the most common strategies are called "skimming the cream" and "penetration pricing". Skimming comes from a strategy of selling the product at a high price and hopefully a high profit level to a small segment of the market that will gladly pay the high price for some reason. When the market has been saturated at the high price, the strategy says to get out of the business or develop a new pricing strategy to generate new business at a lower price.

Penetration pricing recognizes the need to develop a volume of business that will set the stage for future business (getting product trial often leads to adoption) or generating total revenue through volume which leads to profits.

Thus, the pricing strategy needs to be part and parcel of the overall business strategy and not simply based on cost plus some profit percentage, or ROI, or any rule of thumb not tied to your product and its business strategy.

Entry strategy. An important aspect of your marketing strategy is the method of entering the business. A new entrant into a product/market has a number of problems to overcome including being an unknown supplier of an unknown product. Again, look at your company and your product as it relates to the marketplace—what do you need to overcome to be successful and how would you overcome it? No checklist or magic strategy will provide you with a strategy that will be applicable to your company, your new product and your marketplace. Examine all aspects of your marketing strategy for possible entry problems and modify accordingly.

Marketing Strategy in Perspective

The development of marketing strategy requires that you understand the marketplace for your new product, and develop a strategy that will match your product offering with the needs and mechanics of the marketplace. The development of a marketing strategy should receive as much support and attention as any other aspect of your new product program.

A lot of questions have been posed for you to answer regarding your new product and the market for your new product. If there is one basic question that could be asked, it would probably be, "Can you develop a marketing strategy that will take advantage of the uniqueness of your new product and the mechanics of the marketplace for that product?"

What's Next?

The next sections of this book will cover the production planning activity as it impacts upon the new product program.

Production Planning

WHEN YOU PLAN FOR THE PRODUCTION of your new product, consider the overall business opportunity. In many cases, your new product might be produced in the same building and with the same equipment that produces your current product line. In other cases, you may want to subcontract the manufacturing of your new product to an outside company. Or, it might be feasible and advantageous to construct a new facility designed to produce your new product. The decision should be based on an economic analysis of the alternative methods of producing the product as well as an analysis of where your company is headed. What follows is a brief review of production planning from the standpoint of the new product process.

Process Selection

Process selection should be based on a review of the various methods of producing your new product as well as a number of factors involved in selecting between alternative processes. These include:

- capital costs versus operating costs
- expected product life cycle
- potential for growth and expansion

Capital costs versus operating costs. The selection of a production process often involves a trade-off between investing money in capital equipment and cost or labor saving equipment, or investing a lesser amount of money and expecting to end up with higher production costs. This decision is usually based on the current financial condition of the company, the need for short term cash flow, the availability of investment capital, and the current need for short term profits and return on investment.

Expected product life cycle. The expected life of the business associated with your new product will have a lot to do with your decision to invest in a production facility. A new product with an expected life of 3 to 5 years may not warrant the same investment as a product with an expected life of 20 years or more. Again, your economic analysis should reflect the planned life of the business opportunity associated with your new product.

Growth potential. The potential growth of the business associated with your new product may provide a rationale for the selection of a manufacturing process. Some processes are very adaptable to future growth, while others are not. If future growth is an important part of your business plan, a production process adaptable to this growth should be considered.

Cost Estimating

Cost estimating could be the key ingredient in the process selection task. Without good cost estimating, it is difficult to develop any meaningful economic analysis to help make decisions regarding process selection, equipment selection or make/buy decisions.

Cost estimating techniques cannot be fully explored in a book like this. However, there are other sources of information on cost estimating techniques and economic analysis you may refer to. Let it suffice to restate here that cost estimating and economic analysis. The basic criterion should be one of making production process and equipment. It will have a major role in your planning for profitability.

Make Versus Buy

The decision whether to make your product in your own

plant or to purchase the product or components from other manufacturing companies should be made on the basis of an economic analysis. The basic criterion should be one of making a satisfactory return on the money you invest in the manufacturing facility. There are other factors to consider including control over scheduling and quality, but the main point of concern should be the return on the investment in facilities.

Many companies feel that there is something inherently wrong with purchasing parts or components from outside suppliers. But, for a company that is capital short, buying from a subcontractor may be the only feasible alternative. In other cases, there may be real advantages (economic and other) to producing a part or component in your own shop. You should evaluate the potential benefits to your company of both making and buying parts or components.

Plant and Equipment Selection

The selection of plant and equipment is a complicated matter and requires a thorough analysis of alternatives, and a detailed economic analysis. Again, the selection process and criteria should be related to the overall business opportunity and the goals and objectives of your company.

Summary

This section is not intended to provide you with a guide to capital budgeting, cost estimating, production planning, process selection, or any of the host of decisions that must be made relative to the production of your new product. It is important that you seek out experienced advice in those areas where you are a little weak. There is a lot of risk involved in investing many thousands of dollars in a production facility for your new product. One way to reduce the level of risk is to seek out the views and recommendations of experienced production planners and engineers. Another way to reduce the level of risk is to subcontract the production of all or a portion of the product to another company that already has the production facility on stream.

Building a Business

T HIS SECTION WILL DISCUSS some factors that might be important to the profitable growth of your new product venture
in the future. It may also be applicable to the small business
already having several product lines including a new product
recently introduced. Basically, it's all about making a profit and
continuing to make a profit.

Cost Control

In order to generate a profit through the sale of your new
product, you need knowledge of and some control over your
costs of doing business. A system of cost accounting can tell you
enough about your cost structure to allow you to exercise control over it. If everything is hidden in overhead accounts that
bear no relation to the production of your product, you cannot
possibly see what can or should be done to improve your profitability.

Every company has an accounting system for tax purposes.
However, as in other management situations, you will probably
need more detailed information if your accounting system is to
help you determine where problems exist and what to do about
them. For example, the typical income statement looks like this:

sales revenue	xxx
less mfg. cost of goods sold including mfg. overhead	xx
Gross profit	xx
less selling & admin. expenses	xx
Net income before tax	xx

The system that was discussed under the venture analysis section of this book can also be used to understand the cost structure and resultant profit structure of your company. It will require extra work because it cannot be used for tax purposes, but it will allow you to understand and deal with the profit obstacles and opportunities in your company.

This method is the contribution margin and direct costing approach. Under this method the income statement looks like this:

sales revenue	xxx
less variable costs of goods sold	xx
Contribution Margin	xx
less fixed costs	xx
Net income before tax	xx

Contribution margin is the sales revenue less *all variable costs* associated with the production and sale of the product directly. Fixed costs include *all fixed costs* no matter where they come from in the organization. Inventory is carried on the books at *variable costs* only. All fixed costs are expenses during the period they were spent.

The figure on the following page contains a sample income statement for a two division company with costs separated out for each division as well as for four separate products for one of the divisions. Under direct costing, only those costs that can be directly allocated to a specific product are associated with that product. Thus, products are not helped or hindered by allocation procedures. Under this system each product must

TABLE V. *Sample income statement using contribution margin/direct costing procedures*

	Company as a whole	Company breakdown		Not allocable to a product	Division breakdown by Product (B only)			
		Division A	Division B		Product 1	Product 2	Product 3	Product 4
Sales	10000	4000	6000	—	1500	3000	500	1000
Variable cost of manufacturing	6000	2500	3500	—	800	2300	100	300
Manufacturing contribution margin	4000	1500	2500	—	700	700	400	700
Variable selling & admin. costs	1500	500	1000	—	300	300	300	100
Contribution margin	2500	1000	1500	—	400	400	100	600
Fixed cost allocable to divisions [1]	1200	700	500	100	150	150	50	50
Short run margin	1300	300	1000	(100)	250	250	50	550
Other fixed costs [2]	500	200	300	50	50	100	50	50
Division margin	800	100	700	(150)	200	150	0	500
Joint fixed costs	200							
Net income before tax	600							

[1] Advertising, research, supervision, salesmen's salaries

[2] Depreciation, insurance, property taxes, division manager's salary

stand on its own with regard to the money it generates (contribution margin) to pay the fixed costs and profit for your company. Many companies have found that this sort of analysis has identified unprofitable products that were always thought to be winners and has helped to identify the real winners.

Side Shows

Side shows are anything that takes place outside of the normal business that tends to "sap off" resources and detract from the company's ability to conduct business. New products are viewed as possible side shows in many companies, and indeed can become dangerous to the health of your company if you are not careful.

Your new product should not be competing directly with your current businesss and products for valuable resources such as salesmen's time, or production scheduling, or other factors important to the success of not only your new product, but also your entire business. Do everything you can to keep your new products from detracting from existing products while providing them with the resources they need to grow.

Cash Flow

Cash flow planning is critical to the very existence of many companies and especially new companies. Your new product program should carefully examine the cash needs associated with your new product. It may be quite a few months or even years before your new product generates any positive cash flow. Your capital budget for the new product should recognize and plan for these working capital needs.

Pruning

New products that don't "make it" can have a bad effect on your overall company. Don't let someone's ego get in the way of making the decision to drop a product that is a real loser. The concept of sunk costs is applicable here: everything that is spent before right now is sunk and cannot be recovered. Thus, decisions should be based on the future and not based on the level of investments made heretofore. The statement that "we have too much invested in this project to stop now" tends to indicate that more money down the rat hole will somehow make everything OK. Don't get caught in this one. Getting out of a bad product or a bad market or a bad business will have as good of an effect on your bottom line as getting into a good product, a good market, or a good business.

Marketplace Perspective

Much of the thinking that went into the initial development of your new product idea, concept, opportunity model, and marketing strategy was based on an understanding of the marketplace and its needs and wants. Don't lose this perspective after you launch your new product. Keep looking to the marketplace for ideas and feedback on your existing products, new products, and future opportunities. The marketplace is where the action is; you should know it and know it well.

A Ranking Procedure for New Product Opportunities

THE MAIN PROBLEM you will face when trying to come up with a new product idea is to narrow the list of opportunities to find the *relatively best* opportunity. Note the term "relatively best." You are not looking for the perfect opportunity; you have a list and you are attempting to find the best opportunity on that list. What is needed then is a sequential rating operation which rates the opportunities against each other rather than rating the opportunities independently and absolutely. This way you can move from ideas to action.

The basic objective is to start off with a large number (or any number) of candidate ideas. Then, sequentially screen and rank these ideas to reduce the list to a smaller number and so on. Finally, you will end up with several new product ideas that represent the "best" opportunities for new products or new markets.

This sequential screening and ranking procedure requires the formulation of ranking criteria that currently reflects the pros and cons of new products vis–a–vis your company. Criteria should be selected that are easily evaluated with a minimum of outside research. For example, criteria such as:

- minimum R & D required
- extensive sales effort not required
- proprietary opportunity for your company
- non-competitive marketplace

would be examples of criteria that reflect your capabilities and can be easily applied to the screening process.

The process itself[1] requires that each criterion receive a numerical range of 0–10 or 0–5 or 0–3. The range reflects relative importance—more important criterion 0–10 range, less important 0–5, etc. Each of the new product ideas is rated against all other ideas on each criterion and then a total score is determined. Screening criteria should be positive in nature. In other words, a 10 represents the best on the criteria, a 0 the worst. Criteria may be negative; that is, "marketing not important" where a 10 would indicate a product that could sell itself.

Based on total score, the ideas may be ranked and the lower half eliminated while the upper half is to be subjected to further criteria. It is suggested that no more than three criteria be used for any one screening. As the number of ideas is reduced, more complicated criteria such as market size or degree of competition can be applied without creating a research monster.

The goal of the screening process is to reduce the number of ideas to about 2–4 of the "best" ideas which can then be evaluated for further development, investment, and future new product introduction.

The screening process has succeeded in *systematically* and *cheaply* reducing the list of ideas to a number that can be subjected to relatively expensive and time consuming market research techniques.

To eliminate bias, *at least* 3 people should be involved in the sequential process. Unanimous rankings are desirable—that is, the bottom half of each person's list is compared with the others and the consensus dropped. The others are retained for further screening and ranking. Remember the process rates each idea against other ideas—it does *not* rate each idea independently and absolutely against all criteria. *The whole concept is based on finding the best in the list not the absolute best.*

This method will allow you to successfully make the transition from ideas to action, provided you are willing to take one or more of the recommended ideas and actually move to the next steps in the process—the business plan, funding, and action.

---

[1] A sample rating sheet appears at the end of this appendix.

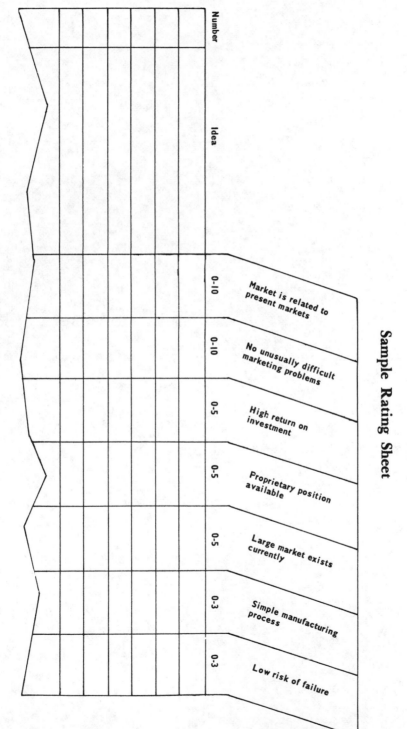

Figure A1.

Sample Rating Sheet

Appendix B

What Is
A Survey?

By Robert Ferber, Chair
Paul Sheatsley
Anthony Turner
Joseph Waksberg

Subcommittee of the Section on Survey Research Methods

Source: American Statistical Association.

Preface

People are accustomed to seeing the results of surveys reported in the daily press, incorporated in advertising claims, and mentioned on numerous occasions by political analysts, social critics, and economic forecasters. Much less frequent, however, is any discussion of the reliability of these surveys or what is involved in carrying them out. The wealth of reported information may easily lull the user into assuming that surveys are easy to undertake, and to overlook the many steps involved in a properly-conducted survey. If technical issues are recognized, there is a frequent tendency to assume that they should be safely left to the survey expert.

In fact, many of the surveys that appear in the daily press are conducted under great time pressure and with insufficient allowance for the many different aspects of the process that need to be controlled. Yet, unless the reader of these survey results is aware of what is involved in a survey, and what quality controls are needed, s(he) is unable to form any opinion of the confidence to be placed in the results, and usually is not even in a position to know what questions to ask about such surveys.

In an effort to fill this gap, the Section on Survey Research Methods of the American Statistical Association appointed a committee to prepare a brochure that would describe survey operations without using technical terminology, and be understandable to interested persons not trained in statistics. The result is the present brochure which, it is hoped, will promote a better understanding of what is involved in carrying out a sample survey, and aspects that have to be taken into account in evaluating the results of surveys.

The American Statistical Association is pleased to publish the report in the hope and expectation that it will prove useful to a wide readership. The association is fortunate to have had four such able statisticians as Robert Ferber, Professor of Economics and Business, Survey Research Laboratory, University of Illinois; Paul Sheatsley, Survey Director, National Opinion Research Center, University of Chicago; Anthony Turner, Chief of International Mathematical-Statistical Staff, Statistical Methods Division, U.S. Bureau of the Census; and Joseph Waksberg, Vice President, Westat, Inc., form the committee that undertook the work. It thanks them for their efforts.

Margaret E. Martin, President
American Statistical Association
1980

Contents

Introduction

The growing popularity of surveys for throwing light on different problems has led to a tendency to overlook the fact that surveys involve many technical problems. Too many surveys seem to be conducted more or less on an ad hoc basis, with the result that the GIGO (garbage in, garbage out) principle is brought into play. This brochure seeks to help the non-statistician to avoid this danger, by providing a nontechnical introduction to sample surveys of human populations and the many different ways in which such surveys are used.

The principal focus is on the design of a survey and on the collection of survey data—two areas in which the many intricacies involved are frequently overlooked. However, attention is also given to the need for proper evaluation of survey data, an essential prerequisite for assessing the value of a survey as well as a basis for proper analysis of the data. (Analysis of survey data is a major topic in itself, and is not covered here.)

This brochure can be used in a variety of ways, such as:

• By statisticians and survey agencies, to give prospective clients some appreciation of what is involved in a sample survey.

• By research executives, to help their nonresearch counterparts understand how surveys are conducted.

• By instructors in introductory social science and other courses, to give students a brief introduction to sample surveys.

• By international agencies and others advising in other countries, to give government officials in these other countries an understanding of the various steps of a sample survey.

It should be stressed that this brochure is *not* intended to provide students of statistics or prospective specialists in the field with a comprehensive understanding of survey methods. For this purpose, the books listed at the end of the brochure need to be used, plus many of the specialized sources dealing with the techniques of survey design and data collection. This brochure is meant for nonspecialists, for the users of survey data. If it leads them to have a better appreciation of what is involved in a sample survey, its purpose will have been served.

Characteristics
of Surveys

The Need

A ny observation or investigation of the facts about a situation
may be called a survey. But today the word is most often
used to describe a method of gathering information from a number of individuals, a "sample," in order to learn something about
the larger population from which the sample has been drawn.
Thus, a sample of voters is surveyed in advance of an election to
determine how the public perceives the candidates and the issues.
A manufacturer makes a survey of the potential market before
introducing a new product. A government agency commissions a
survey to gather the factual information it needs in order to evaluate
existing legislation or draft new legislation. For example, what medical care do people receive, and how is it paid for? Who uses food
stamps? How many people are unemployed?

It has been said that the United States is no longer an industrial society but an "information society." That is, our major problems and tasks no longer focus merely on the production of the
goods and services necessary to our survival and comfort. Rather,
our major problems and tasks today are those of organizing and
managing the incredibly complex efforts required to meet the
needs and wishes of nearly 220 million Americans. To do this
requires a prompt and accurate flow of information on preferences,
needs and behavior. It is in response to this critical need for information on the part of the government, business and social institutions that so much reliance is placed upon surveys.

Surveys come in many different forms and have a wide variety of purposes, but they do have certain characteristics in common. Unlike a census, they gather information from only a small sample of people (or farms, businesses or other units, depending on the purpose of the study). In a bonafide survey, the sample is not selected haphazardly or only from persons who volunteer to participate. It is scientifically chosen so that each individual in the population has a known chance of selection. In this way, the results can be reliably projected to the larger public.

Information is collected by means of standardized questions so that every individual surveyed responds to exactly the same question. The survey's intent is not to describe the particular individuals who by chance are part of the sample, but to obtain a statistical profile of the population. Individual respondents are never identified and the survey's results are presented in the form of summaries, such as statistical tables and charts.

The sample size required for a survey will depend on the reliability needed which, in turn, depends on how the results will be used. Consequently, there is no simple rule for sample size that can be used for all surveys. However, analysts usually find that a moderate sample size is sufficient for most needs. For example, the well-known national polls generally use samples of about 1,500 persons to reflect national attitudes and opinions. A sample of this size produces accurate estimates even for a country as large as the United States with a population of over 200 million.

When it is realized that a properly selected sample of only 1,500 individuals can reflect various characteristics of the total population within a very small margin of error, it is easy to understand the value of surveys in a complex society such as ours. They provide a speedy and economical means of determining facts about our economy and people's knowledge, attitudes, beliefs, expectations, and behavior.

Who Does Surveys?

We all know of the public opinion polls which are reported in the press and broadcast media. The Gallup Poll and the Harris Survey issue reports periodically, describing national public opinion on a wide range of current issues. State polls and metropolitan area polls, often supported by a local newspaper or TV station, are reported regularly in many localities. The major broadcasting networks and national news magazines also conduct polls and report their findings.

But the great majority of surveys are not exposed to public

view. The reason is that, unlike the public opinion polls, most surveys are directed to a specific administrative or commercial purpose. The wide variety of issues with which surveys deal is illustrated by the following listing of actual uses:

1. The U.S. Department of Agriculture conducted a survey to find out how poor people use food stamps.

2. Major TV networks rely on surveys to tell them how many and what types of people are watching their programs.

3. Auto manufacturers use surveys to find out how satisfied people are with their cars.

4. The U.S. Bureau of the Census conducts a survey every month to obtain information on employment and unemployment in the nation.

5. The National Center for Health Statistics sponsors a survey every year to determine how much money people are spending for different types of medical care.

6. Local housing authorities make surveys to ascertain satisfaction of people in public housing with their living accommodations.

7. The Illinois Board of Higher Education surveys the interest of Illinois residents in adult education.

8. Local transportation authorities conduct surveys to acquire information on people's commuting and travel habits.

9. Magazine and trade journals utilize surveys to find out what their subscribers are reading.

10. Surveys are used to ascertain what sort of people use our national parks and other recreation facilities.

Surveys of human populations also provide an important source of basic social science knowledge. Economists, psychologists, political scientists and sociologists obtain foundation or government grants to study such matters as income and expenditure patterns among households, the roots of ethnic or racial prejudice, comparative voting behavior, or the effects of employment of women on family life. (Surveys are also made of nonhuman populations, such as of animals, soils and housing; they are not discussed here, although many of the principles are the same.)

Moreover, once collected, survey data can be analyzed and reanalyzed in many different ways. Data tapes with identification of individuals removed can be made available for analysis by community groups, scientific researchers and others.

Types of Surveys

Surveys can be classified in a number of ways. One dimension is by size and type of sample. Many surveys study the total adult population, but others might focus on special population groups: physicians, community leaders, the unemployed, or users of a particular product or service. Surveys may be conducted on a national, state or local basis, and may seek to obtain data from a few hundred or many thousand people.

Surveys can also be classified by their method of data collection. Thus, there are mail surveys, telephone surveys, and personal interview surveys. There are also newer methods of data collection by which information is recorded directly into computers. This includes measurement of TV audiences carried out by devices attached to a sample of TV sets which automatically record in a computer the channels being watched. Mail surveys are seldom used to collect information from the general public because names and addresses are not often available and the response rate tends to be low, but the method may be highly effective with members of particular groups; for example, subscribers to a specialized magazine or members of a professional association. Telephone interviewing is an efficient method of collecting some types of data and is being increasingly used. A personal interview in a respondent's home or office is much more expensive than a telephone survey but is necessary when complex information is to be collected.

Some surveys combine various methods. Survey workers may use the telephone to "screen" for eligible respondents (say, women of a particular age group) and then make appointments for a personal interview. Some information, such as the characteristics of the respondent's home, may be obtained by observation rather than questioning. Survey data are also sometimes obtained by self-administered questionnaires filled out by respondents in groups, e.g., a class of school children or a group of shoppers in a central location.

One can further classify surveys by their content. Some surveys focus on opinions and attitudes (such as a pre-election survey of voters), while others are concerned with factual characteristics or behavior (such as a survey of people's health, housing or transportation habits). Many surveys combine questions of both types. Thus, a respondent will be asked if s(he) has heard or read about an issue, what s(he) knows about it, his (her) opinion, how strongly s(he) feels and why, interest in the issue, past experience with it, and also certain factual information which will help the survey analyst classify the responses (such as age, sex, marital status, occupation, and place of residence).

The questions may be open-ended ("Why do you feel that way?") or closed ("Do you approve or disapprove?"); they may ask the respondent to rate a political candidate or a product on some kind of scale; they may ask for a ranking of various alternatives. The questionnaire may be very brief—a few questions taking five minutes or less, or it can be quite long—requiring an hour or more of the respondent's time. Since it is inefficient to identify and approach a large national sample for only a few items of information, there are "omnibus" surveys which combine the interests of several clients in a single interview. In such surveys, the respondent will be asked a dozen questions on one subject, half a dozen more on another subject, and so on.

Because changes in attitude or behavior cannot be reliably ascertained from a single interview, some surveys employ a "panel design," in which the same respondents are interviewed two or more times. Such surveys are often used during election campaigns, or to chart a family's health or purchasing pattern over a period of time. They are also used to trace changes in behavior over time, as with the social experiments that study changes by low-income families in work behavior in response to an income maintenance plan.

What Sort of People Work on Surveys?

The survey worker best known to the public is the interviewer who calls on the phone, appears at the door, or stops people at a shopping center. Though survey interviewing may occasionally require long days in the field, it is normally part-time occasional work and is thus well suited for individuals who do not seek full-time employment or who wish to supplement their regular income. Previous experience is not usually required for an interviewing job. Most research companies will provide their own basic training for the task. The main requirements are an ability to approach strangers, to persuade them to participate in the survey, and to conduct the interview in exact accordance with instructions.

Behind the interviewers are the in-house research staff who design the survey, determine the sample design, develop the questionnaire, supervise the data collection, carry out the clerical and computer operations necessary to process the completed interviews, analyze the data, and write the reports. In most survey research agencies, the senior people will have taken courses in survey methods at the graduate level and will hold advanced degrees in sociology, statistics, marketing, or psychology, or they will have the equivalent in business experience. Middle-level supervisors and research associates frequently have similar academic backgrounds, or they have advanced out of the ranks of clerks, interviewers or coders on the basis of their competence and experience.

Are Responses Confidential?

The privacy of the information supplied by survey respondents is of prime concern to all reputable survey organizations. At the U.S. Bureau of the Census, for example, the confidentiality of the data collected is protected by law (Title 13 of the U.S. Code). In Canada, the Statistics Act guarantees the confidentiality of data collected by Statistics Canada, and other countries have similar safeguards. Also, a number of professional organizations that rely on survey methods have codes of ethics that prescribe rules for keeping survey responses confidential. The recommended policy for survey organizations to safeguard such confidentiality includes:

1. Using only code numbers for the identity of a respondent on a questionnaire, and keeping the code separate from that of the questionnaires.

2. Refusing to give names and addresses of survey respondents to anybody outside of the survey organization, including clients.

3. Destroying questionnaires and identifying information about respondents after the responses have been put onto computer tape.

4. Omitting the names and addresses of survey respondents from computer tapes used for analysis.

5. Presenting statistical tabulations by broad enough categories that individual respondents cannot be singled out.

How a Survey
Is Carried Out

A s noted earlier, a survey usually has its beginnings when an individual or institution is confronted with an information need and there are no existing data which suffice. A politician may wish to tap prevailing voter opinions in his district about a proposal to build a superhighway through the county. A government agency may wish to assess the impact on the primary recipients and their families of one of its social welfare programs. A university researcher may wish to examine the relationship between actual voting behavior and expressed opinion on some political issue or social concern.

Designing a Survey

Once the information need has been identified and a determination made that existing data are inadequate, the first step in planning a survey is to lay out the objectives of the investigation. This is generally the function of the sponsor of the inquiry. The objectives should be as specific, clear-cut and unambiguous as possible. The required accuracy level of the data has a direct bearing on the overall survey design. For example, in a sample survey whose main purpose is to estimate the unemployment rate for a city, the approximate number of persons to be sampled can be estimated mathematically when one knows the amount of sampling error that can be tolerated in the survey results.

Given the objectives, the methodology for carrying out the survey is developed. A number of interrelated activities are involved. Rules must be formulated for defining and locating eligible respondents, the method of collecting the data must be decided upon, a questionnaire must be designed and pretested, procedures must be developed for minimizing or controlling response errors, appropriate samples must be designed and selected, interviewers must be hired and trained (except for surveys involving self-administered questionnaires), plans must be made for handling nonresponse cases, and tabulation and analysis must be performed.

Designing the questionnaire represents one of the most critical stages in the survey development process, and social scientists have given a great deal of thought to issues involved in questionnaire design. The questionnaire links the information need to the realized measurement.

Unless the concepts are clearly defined and the questions unambiguously phrased, the resulting data are apt to contain serious biases. In a survey to estimate the incidence of robbery victimization, for example, one might want to ask, "Were you robbed during the last six months?" Though apparently straightforward and clearcut, the question does present an ambiguous stimulus. Many respondents are unaware of the legal distinction between robbery (involving personal confrontation of the victim by the offender) and burglary (involving breaking and entering but no confrontation), and confuse the two in a survey. In the National Crime Survey, conducted by the Bureau of the Census, the questions on robbery victimization do not mention "robbery." Instead, several questions are used which, together, seek to capture the desired responses by using more universally understood phrases that are consistent with the operational definition of robbery.

Designing a suitable questionnaire entails more than well-defined concepts and distinct phraseology. Attention must also be given to its length, for unduly long questionnaires are burdensome to the respondent, are apt to induce respondent fatigue and hence response errors, refusals, and incomplete questionnaires, and may contribute to higher nonresponse rates in subsequent surveys involving the same respondents. Several other factors must be taken into account when designing a questionnaire to minimize or prevent biasing the results and to facilitate its use both in the field and in the processing center. They include such diverse considerations as the sequencing of sections or individual questions in the document, the inclusion of check boxes or precoded answer categories versus open-ended questions, the questionnaire's physical size and format, and instructions to the respondent or to the interviewer on whether certain questions are to be skipped depending on response patterns to prior questions.

Selecting the proper respondent in a sample unit is a key element in survey planning. For surveys where the inquiry is basically factual in nature, any knowledgeable person associated with the sample unit may be asked to supply the needed information. This procedure is used in the Current Population Survey, where the sample units are households and any responsible adult in a household is expected to be able to provide accurate answers on the employment-unemployment status of the eligible household members.

In other surveys, a so-called "household" respondent will produce erroneous and/or invalid information. For example, in attitude surveys it is generally accepted that a randomly chosen respondent from among the eligible household members produces a more valid cross section of opinion than does the nonrandomly selected household repondent. This is because a nonrandomly selected individual acting as household respondent is more likely to be someone who is at home during the day, and the working public and their attitudes would be underrepresented.

Another important feature of the survey planning process is devising ways to keep response errors and biases to a minimum. These considerations depend heavily on the subject matter of the survey. For example, memory plays an important role in surveys dealing with past events that the respondent is expected to report accurately, such as in a consumer expenditure survey. In such retrospective surveys, therefore, an appropriate choice of reference period must be made so that the respondent is not forced to report events that may have happened too long ago to remember accurately. In general, attention must be given to whether the questions are too sensitive, whether they may prejudice the respondent, whether they unduly invade the respondent's privacy, and whether the information sought is too difficult even for a willing respondent to provide. Each of these concerns has an important bearing on the overall validity of the survey results.

Sampling Aspects

Virtually all surveys that are taken seriously by social scientists and policy makers use some form of scientific sampling. Even the decennial Censuses of Population and Housing use sampling techniques for gathering the bulk of the data items, although 100 percent enumeration is used for the basic population counts. Methods of sampling are well-grounded in statistical theory and in the theory of probability. Hence, reliable and efficient estimates of a needed statistic can be made by surveying a carefully constructed sample of a population, as opposed to the entire population, provided of course that a large proportion of the sample members give the requested information.

The particular type of sample used depends on the objectives and scope of the survey, including the overall survey budget, the method of data collection, the subject matter and the kind of respondent needed. A first step, however, in deciding on an appropriate sampling method is to define the relevant population. This target population can be all the people in the entire nation or all the people in a certain city, or it can be a subset such as all teenagers in a given location. The population of interest need not be people; it may be wholesale businesses or institutions for the handicapped or government agencies, and so on.

The types of samples range from simple random selection of the population units to highly complex samples involving multiple stages or levels of selection with stratification and/or clustering of the units into various groupings. Whether simple or complex, the distinguishing characteristics of a properly designed sample are that all the units in the target population have a known, nonzero chance of being included in the sample, and the sample design is described in sufficient detail to permit reasonably accurate calculation of sampling errors. It is these features that make it scientifically valid to draw inferences from the sample results about the entire population which the sample represents.

Ideally, the sample size chosen for a survey should be based on how reliable the final estimates must be. In practice, usually a trade-off is made between the ideal sample size and the expected cost of the survey. The complexity of a sample plan often depends on the availability of auxiliary information that can be used to introduce efficiencies into the overall design. For example, in a recent Federal Government survey on characteristics of health-care institutions, existing information about the type of care provided and the number of beds in each institution was useful in sorting the institutions into "strata," or groups by type and size, in advance of selecting the sample. The procedure permitted more reliable survey estimates than would have been possible if a simple random selection of institutions had been made without regard to size or type.

A critical element in sample design and selection is defining the source of materials from which a sample can be chosen. This source, termed the sampling frame, generally is a list of some kind, such as a list of housing units in a city, a list of retail establishments in a county or a list of students in a university. The sampling frame can also consist of geographic areas with well-defined natural or artificial boundaries, when no suitable list of the target population exists. In the latter instance, a sample of geographic areas (referred to as segments) is selected and an interviewer canvasses the sample "area segments" and lists the appropriate units—households, retail stores or whatever—so that some or all of them can be designated for inclusion in the final sample.

The sampling frame can also consist of less concrete things, such as all possible permutations of integers that make up banks of telephone numbers, in the case of telephone surveys that seek to include unlisted numbers. The quality of the sampling frame—whether it is up-to-date and how complete—is probably the dominant feature for ensuring adequate coverage of the desired population.

Conducting a Survey

Though a survey design may be well conceived, the preparatory work would be futile if the survey were executed improperly. For personal or telephone interview surveys, interviewers must be carefully trained in the survey's concepts, definitions, and procedures. This may take the form of classroom training, self-study, or both. The training stresses good interviewer techniques on such points as how to make initial contacts, how to conduct interviews in a professional manner and how to avoid influencing or biasing responses. The training generally involves practice interviews to familiarize the interviewers with the variety of situations they are likely to encounter. Survey materials must be prepared and issued to each interviewer, including ample copies of the questionnaire, a reference manual, information about the identification and location of the sample units, and any cards or pictures to be shown to the respondent.

Before conducting the interview, survey organizations frequently send an advance letter to the sample member explaining the survey's purpose and the fact that an interviewer will be calling soon. In many surveys, especially those sponsored by the Federal Government, information must be given to the respondent regarding the voluntary or mandatory nature of the survey, and how the answers are to be used.

Visits to sample units are scheduled with attention to such considerations as the best time of day to call or visit and the number of allowable callbacks for no-one-at-home situations. Controlling the quality of the field work is an essential aspect of good survey practice. This is done in a number of ways, most often through observation or rechecking of a subsample of interviews by supervisory or senior personnel, and through office editing procedures to check for omissions or obvious mistakes in the data.

When the interviews have been completed and the questionnaires filled out, they must be processed in a form so that aggregated totals, averages or other statistics can be computed. This will involve clerical coding of questionnaire items which are not already precoded. Occupation and industry categorizations are typical examples of fairly complex questionnaire coding that is usually done clerically. Also procedures must be developed for coding open-ended questions and for handling items that must be transcribed from one part of the questionnaire to another.

Coded questionnaires are keypunched, entered directly onto tape so that a computer file can be created, or entered directly into the computer. Decisions may then be needed on how to treat missing data and "not answered" items.

Coding, keypunching and transcription operations are subject to human error and must be rigorously controlled through verification processes, either on a sample basis or 100 percent basis. Once a computer file has been generated, additional computer editing, as distinct from clerical editing of the data, can be accomplished to alter inconsistent or impossible entries, e.g., a six-year-old grandfather.

When a "clean" file has been produced, the survey data are in a form where analysts can specify to a computer programmer the frequency counts, cross-tabulations or more sophisticated methods of data presentation or computation that are needed to help answer the concerns outlined when the survey was initially conceived.

The results of the survey are usually communicated in publications and in verbal presentations at staff briefings or more formal meetings. Secondary analysis is also often possible to those other than the survey staff by making available computer data files at nominal cost.

Shortcuts to Avoid

As we have seen, conducting a creditable survey entails scores of activities, each of which must be carefully planned and controlled. Taking shortcuts can invalidate the results and badly mislead the user. Four types of shortcuts that crop up often are failure to use a proper sampling procedure, no pretest of the field procedures, failure to follow up nonrespondents and inadequate quality control.

One way to ruin an otherwise well-conceived survey is to use a convenience sample rather than one which is based on a probability design. It may be simple and cheap, for example, to select a sample of names from a telephone directory to find out which candidate people intend to vote for. However, this sampling procedure could give incorrect results since persons without telephones or with unlisted numbers would have no chance to be reflected in the sample, and their voting preferences could be quite different from persons who have listed telephones. This is what happened with the *Literary Digest* presidential poll of 1936 when use of lists of telephone owners, magazine subscribers and car owners led to a prediction that President Roosevelt would lose the election.

A pretest of the questionnaire and field procedures is the only way of finding out if everything "works," especially if a survey employs a new procedure or a new set of questions. Since it is rarely possible to foresee all the possible misunderstandings or biasing effects of different questions and procedures, it is vital for a well-designed survey plan to include provision for a pretest. This is usually a small-scale pilot study to test the feasibility of the intended techniques or to perfect the questionnaire concepts and wording.

Failure to follow up nonrespondents can ruin an otherwise well-designed survey, for it is not uncommon for the initial response rate to most surveys to be under 50 percent. Plans must include returning to sample households where no one was home, attempting to persuade persons who are inclined to refuse and, in the case of mail surveys, contacting all or a subsample of the nonrespondents by telephone or personal visit to obtain a completed questionnaire. A low response rate does more damage in rendering a survey's results questionable than a small sample, since there is no valid way of scientifically inferring the characteristics of the population represented by the nonrespondents.

Quality control, in the sense of checking the different facets of a survey, enters in at all stages—checking sample selection, verifying interviews and checking the editing and coding of the responses, among other things. In particular, sloppy execution of the survey in the field can seriously damage the results. Without proper quality control, errors can occur with disastrous results, such as selecting or visiting the wrong household, failing to ask questions properly, or recording the incorrect answer. Insisting on proper standards in recruitment and training of interviewers helps a great deal, but equally important is proper review, verification and other quality control measures to ensure that the execution of a survey corresponds to its design.

Using the Results
of a Survey

How Good is the Survey?

The statistics derived from a survey will rarely correspond exactly with the unknown truth. (Whether "true" values always exist is not important in the present context. For fairly simple measurements—the average age of the population, the amount of livestock on farms, etc.—the concept of a true value is fairly straightforward. Whether true values exist for measurements of such items as attitudes toward political candidates, I.Q.'s, etc., is a more complex matter.)

Fortunately, the value of a statistic does not depend on its being exactly true. To be useful, a statistic need not be exact, but it does need to be sufficiently reliable to serve the particular needs. No overall criterion of reliability applies to all surveys since the margin of error that can be tolerated in a study depends on the actions or recommendations that will be influenced by the data. For example, economists examining unemployment rates consider a change of 0.2 percent as having an important bearing on the United States economy. Consequently, in the official United States surveys used to estimate unemployment, an attempt is made to keep the margin of error below 0.2 percent. Conversely, there are occasions when a high error rate is acceptable. Sometimes a city will conduct a survey to measure housing vacancies to determine if there is a tight housing supply. If the true vacancy rate is very low, say one percent, survey results that show double this percentage will not do any harm; any results in the range of zero to two or three percent will lead to the same conclusion—a tight housing market.

In many situations the tolerable error will depend on the kind of result expected. For example, during presidential elections the major television networks obtain data on election night from a sample of election precincts, in order to predict the election results early in the evening. In a state in which a large difference is expected (pre-election polls may indicate that one candidate leads by a substantial majority and is likely to receive 60 percent of the vote), even with an error of five or six percent it would still be possible to predict the winner with a high probability of being correct. A relatively small sample size may be adequate in such a state. However, much more precise estimates are required in states where the two candidates are fairly evenly matched and where, say, a 52–48 percent vote is expected.

Thus, no general rule can be laid down to determine the reliability that would apply to all surveys. It is necessary to consider the purpose of the particular study, how the data will be used, and the effect of errors of various sizes on the action taken based on the survey results. These factors will affect the sample size, the design of the questionnaire, the effort put into training and supervising the interview staff, and so on. Estimates of error also need to be considered in analyzing and interpreting the results of the survey.

Sources of Errors

In evaluating the accuracy of a survey, it is convenient to distinguish two sources of errors: 1. sampling errors, and 2. nonsampling errors, including the effect of refusals and not-at-homes, respondents providing incorrect information, coding or other processing errors, and clerical errors in sampling.

Sampling errors

Good survey practice includes calculation of sampling errors, which is possible if probability methods are used in selecting the sample. Furthermore, information on sampling errors should be made readily available to all users of the statistics. If the survey results are published, data on sampling errors should be included in the publication. If information is disseminated in other ways, other means of informing the public are necessary. Thus, it is not uncommon to hear television newscasters report on the size of sampling errors as part of the results of some polling activity.

There are a number of ways of describing and presenting data on sampling errors so that users can take them into account. For example, in a survey designed to produce only a few statistics (such as the votes that the candidates for a particular office are expected to get), the results could be stated that Candidate A's votes are estimated at 57 percent with the error unlikely to be more than 3 percent, so that this candidate's votes are expected to fall in the range of 54–60 percent. Other examples can be found in most publications of the principal statistical agencies of the United States Government, such as the Bureau of the Census.

Nonsampling errors

Unfortunately, unlike sampling errors, there is no simple and direct method of estimating the size of nonsampling errors. In most surveys, it is not practical to measure the possible effect on the statistics of the various potential sources of error. However, in the past 30 or 40 years, there has been a considerable amount of research on the kinds of errors that are likely to arise in different kinds of surveys. By examining the procedures and operations of a specific survey, experienced survey statisticians will frequently be able to assess its quality. Rarely will this produce actual error ranges, as for sampling errors. In most cases, the analyst can only state that, for example, the errors are probably relatively small and will not affect most conclusions drawn from the survey, or that the errors may be fairly large and inferences are to be made with caution.

Nonsampling errors can be classified into two groups—random types or errors whose effects approximately cancel out if fairly large samples are used, and biases which tend to create errors in the same direction and thus cumulate over the entire sample. With large samples, the possible biases are the principal causes for concern about the quality of a survey.

Biases can arise from any aspect of the survey operation. Some of the main contributing causes of bias are:

1. *Sampling operations.* There may be errors in sample selection, or part of the population may be omitted from the sampling frame, or weights to compensate for disproportionate sampling rates may be omitted.

2. *Noninterviews.* Information is generally obtained for only part of the sample. Frequently there are differences between the non-

interview population and those interviewed.

3. *Adequacy of respondent.* Sometimes respondents cannot be interviewed and information is obtained about them from others, but the "proxy" respondent is not always as knowledgeable about the facts.

4. *Understanding the concepts.* Some respondents may not understand what is wanted.

5. *Lack of knowledge.* Respondents in some cases do not know the information requested, or do not try to obtain the correct information.

6. *Concealment of the truth.* Out of fear or suspicion of the survey, respondents may conceal the truth. In some instances, this concealment may reflect a respondent's desire to answer in a way that is socially acceptable, such as indicating that s(he) is carrying out an energy conservation program when this is not actually so.

7. *Loaded questions.* The question may be worded to influence the respondents to answer in a specific (not necessarily correct) way.

8. *Processing errors.* These can include coding errors, data keying, computer programming errors, etc.

9. *Conceptual problems.* There may be differences between what is desired and what the survey actually covers. For example, the population or the time period may not be the one for which information is needed, but had to be used to meet a deadline.

10. *Interviewer errors.* Interviewers may misread the question or twist the answers in their own words and thereby introduce bias.

Obviously, each survey is not necessarily subject to all these sources of error. However, a good survey statistician will explore all of these possibilities. It is considered good practice to report on the percent of the sample that could not be interviewed, and as many of the other factors listed as practicable.

Budgeting
a Survey

We have seen from the preceding sections that many different stages are involved in a survey. These include tasks such as planning, sample design, sample selection, questionnaire preparation, pretesting, interviewer hiring and training, data collection, data reduction, data processing, and report preparation. From a time point of view, these different stages are not necessarily additive since many of them overlap. This is illustrated in the attached diagram which portrays the sequence of steps involved in a typical personal interview survey. Some steps, such as sample design and listing housing units in the areas to be covered in the survey, can be carried out at the same time a questionnaire is being revised and put into final form. Although they are not additive, all of these steps are time-consuming, and one of the most common errors is to underestimate the time needed by making a global estimate without considering these individual stages.

How much time is needed for a survey? This varies with the type of survey and the particular situation. Sometimes a survey can be done in two or three weeks, if it involves a brief questionnaire, and if the data are to be collected by telephone from a list already available. More usually, however, a survey of several hundred or a few thousand individuals will take anywhere from a few months to more than a year, from initial planning to having results ready for analysis.

A flow diagram for a particular survey is very useful in estimating the cost of such a survey. Such a diagram ensures that allow-

STAGES OF A SURVEY

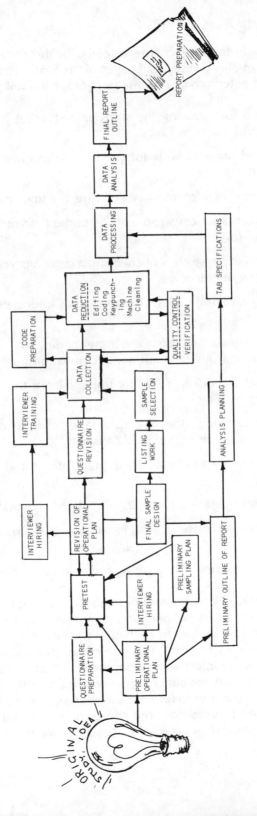

ance is made for the expense involved in the different tasks, as well as for quality checks at all stages of the work. Thus, among the factors that enter into an expense budget are the following:

1. Staff time for planning the study and steering it through the various stages.

2. Labor and material costs for pretesting the questionnaire and field procedures.

3. Supervisory costs for interviewer hiring, training and supervision.

4. Interviewer labor costs and travel expense (and meals and lodging, if out-of-town).

5. Labor and expense costs of checking a certain percentage of the interviews (by reinterviews).

6. Cost of preparing codes for transferring information from the questionnaire.

7. Labor and material costs for editing, coding and keypunching the information from the questionnaire onto computer tape.

8. Cost of spot-checking to assure the quality of the editing, coding and keypunching.

9. Cost of "cleaning" the final data tapes, that is, checking the tapes for inconsistent or impossible answers.

10. Programming costs for preparing tabulations and special analyses of the data.

11. Computer time for the various tabulations and analyses.

12. Labor time and material costs for analysis of the data and report preparation.

13. Telephone charges, postage, reproduction and printing costs.

An integral part of a well-designed survey, both in terms of time and of costs is allowance for quality checks all along the way. For example, checks have to be made that the sample was selected according to specifications, that the interviewers did their work properly, that the information from the questionnaires was coded accurately, that the keypunching was done correctly, and that the computer programs used for data analysis work properly. For these reasons, a good survey does not come cheap, although some are more economical than others. As a rule, surveys made by personal interview are more expensive than by mail or by telephone; and costs will increase with the complexity of the questionnaire and the amount of analysis to be carried out. Also, surveys that involve more interviews tend to be cheaper on a per interview basis than surveys with fewer interviews. This is particularly so where the sample size is less than about a thousand because "tooling up" is involved for just about any survey, except one that is to be repeated on the same group.

Where to Get More Information

S everal professional organizations have memberships heavily involved in survey research. They also frequently have workshops or sessions on surveys as parts of their regional and annual meetings. The principal organizations are the following:

1. The *American Statistical Association* is concerned with survey techniques and with general application of survey data. It has a separate Section on Survey Research Methods which sponsors sessions on surveys at the annual meetings of the association. The many chapters of the association in the various parts of the country also periodically have meetings and workshops on survey methods, and its publications, the *Journal of the American Statistical Association* and the *American Statistician,* carry numerous articles about surveys.

2. The *American Marketing Association* is concerned, among other things, with the application of survey methods to marketing problems. Like the American Statistical Association, it sponsors sessions on survey methods at its annual meetings, and still other sessions are sponsored by its local chapters. Its publications, the *Journal of Marketing* and the *Journal of Marketing Research,* frequently contain articles on surveys.

3. The *American Association for Public Opinion Research* focuses on survey methods as applied to social and media problems. Its journal, the *Public Opinion Quarterly,* regularly carries articles on

survey techniques and on the application of survey methods to political and social problems.

A number of other professional associations in North America place emphasis periodically on survey methods, for example, the Statistical Society of Canada, the American Sociological Association, the American Political Science Association, the Association for Consumer Research, the American Public Health Association, the American Psychological Association, and the Canadian Psychological Association. There are also various business oriented associations such as the Advertising Research Foundation and the American Association of Advertising Agencies, that give attention to survey methods as applied to business. These and other associations publish a number of journals that carry a great deal of material on survey methods.

There are many good books on survey methods written for nontechnical readers. A few of these are:

1. Tanur, Judith, et al., *Statistics: A Guide to the Unknown*. San Francisco: Holden-Day Pub. Co., 1972.

2. Hauser, Philip, *Social Statistics in Use*. New York: Russell Sage Foundation, 1975.

3. Williams, William H., *A Sampler on Sampling*. New York: John Wiley & Sons, 1978.

For further information, contact . . .

Executive Director
American Statistical Association
806 15th Street, N.W.
Washington, D.C. 20005